LEXINGTON HIGH SCHOOL'S

2:25 P.M.

LEXINGTON HIGH SCHOOL'S

2:25 P.M.

◆

Poetry and Prose
from Every Student in the Class

EDITORS: Anthony Tedesco, Karen Russell, Scott Webber,
James Keefe and Angelia Jack

Writers Club Press
San Jose New York Lincoln Shanghai

CONTRIBUTING EDITORS: Jessica Page, Corvis Catsouphes, Elizabeth Crowell, Karen Mechem, Ben Mendales, Richard Russell, Tony Tedesco, Paul Tedesco, Rocio Martinez, Jake Cooney, Jessica Salmons, Colleen Kirisitz, Michelle Manzanares, Ian Alex, Britta Steiner, Mark Palmer, Melinda Anderson, Charles Ginsberg, Amy Finucane, Thomas Elia, Peter Fiumara, Brad Barnes, Todd Barnes, Brent Pickett, James Meyer and Tony Sacco. Thank you for your editorial direction and contributions, proofreading, and production services.

CONTRIBUTORS: Leslie Nicholson, Anne Sanderson, Anne Mikulski, Vito LaMura, Barbara Shapiro, Kevin Murray, Jim Reese and Harvard University's Project Zero, and Dr. Vincenne Revilla Beltran. Thank you for your inspiration, project direction and assistance.

WITH DESIGN, PR AND MARKETING SERVICES FROM
Strong Bat Productions/61 East 8th St., Ste 272, NYC 10003/StrongBat.com)

AND GENEROUS FINANCIAL AND FORMATIVE SUPPORT FROM
Lexington High School Principal Dr. Ernest Van B. Seasholes and
Lexington High School Yearbook Advisor Karen Mechem

THE 2:25 P.M. BOOK SERIES IS PART OF THE STUDENT PUBLISHING PROGRAM
SEE WWW.225PM.ORG FOR MORE INFORMATION AND OUR FREE ONLINE
LITERARY MAGAZINE

Contents

1

◆

ABOUT 2:25 P.M. AND THE STUDENT PUBLISHING PROGRAM

Mission Statement and Objectives for the Student Publishing Program

The Student Publishing Program aims to be a national nonprofit creative writing program which gives secondary students the writing skills and confidence needed to be published, and then secures the professional publication of their compositions—one piece of poetry or prose from every single student—in a network of online literary magazines and a series of paperback books available in bookstores nationwide. One hundred percent of royalties from each school's book sales will help fund future program participation for that school's students.

The Student Publishing Program supports language arts standards and benchmarks through in-class workshops with professional writers and supplementary online learning. The publications will also help students at all learning levels demonstrate their academic merit—to themselves and to the community at-large—beyond grades and standardized test scores.

These student books and magazines are not vanity publications. They're educational tools which also reflect the latest evolution in publishing. The advent of the Internet, e-books and print-on-demand technology has enabled professional writers to publish and market their work directly to readers, and reap far greater benefits from sales. The concept of quality writing has finally moved beyond what big business deems mass market to whatever individual writers and readers deem meaningful.

We've titled the first publication of our pilot effort *2:25 P.M.* because the 2:25 p.m. dismissal bell is the moment of transition between school and the real world, and the Student Publishing Program seeks to bridge that gap, to give real-world purpose and recognition to classroom writing.

STUDENT PUBLISHING PROGRAM OBJECTIVES:

• Help students demonstrate their academic merit—to themselves and to the community at-large—beyond grades and standardized test scores, and help teachers gain recognition for classroom achievements.

• Promote each publication to help students connect and communicate with the widest possible audience beyond their classrooms. Successful promotion will also help fund future participation for each school by increasing its book sales, and involve the whole community in its students' pursuit of local and national education goals.

• Increase student interest in reading by publishing books and magazines written by their true contemporaries—their fellow teenagers who are experiencing similar challenges and heartbreaks and successes. The Student Publishing Program also seeks to publish, translate and organize reading exchanges with schools worldwide to help America's students connect with teenagers from other countries.

• Archive compositions online so students can begin building permanent online portfolios to support their college and job applications, as well as their future publishing efforts.

• Give students the confidence, skills, published clips and resources needed to write for publication *beyond* the Student Publishing Program, including free access to the largest database of student publishing opportunities worldwide—current youth-receptive venues, writing contests, awards and individual state writing grants.

• Support teachers by enriching their language arts programs with our in-class workshops by professional writers—well-qualified individuals who are interested in teaching and may choose to become teachers through our nation's recent New Teacher Program. The Student Publishing Program also aims to help teachers by providing their students with an alternative resource for class and homework questions—an innovative and engaging website with comprehensive language arts curriculum support accessible 24 hours a day.

• Provide the Student Publishing Program to all of America's K-12 schools by securing funding through grants, corporate sponsorships and private donors. These educational literary books and magazines would become as ubiquitous as school yearbooks, but far more beneficial to each student's transition into college and the real world.

For more information about our mission statement and objectives—or to get involved with the Student Publishing Program in any way—please visit 225pm.org or email Anthony Tedesco (anthony@225pm.org).

Introduction from Anthony Tedesco

Writer and Editor

Cofounder of the Student Publishing Program

That last official-looking page was supposed to be my introduction, but it got so official-looking that I finally just labeled it "Mission Statement." Which leaves me with this big blank page and literally 10 minutes to make it less blank before the *2:25 P.M.* manuscript is due. Slightly harrowing for such a sleep-deprived me, but definitely apropos. Lesson #446B of the Student Publishing Program is to dive right into those daunting blank pages and trust that Ms./Mr. Muse will eventually turn up in the mediocre frenzy of streaming words. (Still not here yet.)

My remaining nine-minute introduction deadline is also fitting because *2:25 P.M.* and its sister online literary magazine at 225pm.org are both skeleton-staffed pilot efforts of semi-monumental proportion. Efforts that we're still, of course, very proud of, especially for their semi-monumental potential. But they're definitely the promising tips of the proverbial (two-tipped) iceberg, the frenetically produced seedlings/600-other-metaphors for how beneficial a fully funded Student Publishing Program could be for K–12 students nationwide.

As long as I've already used the word "proud" in a sentence, I'd also like to say that I'm proud we've started the Student Publishing Program at Lexington High School. Not only because I'm a New York City boy with Lexington roots, an LHS diploma circa 1987, and two of the best parents in the whole parental world living right here in Lexington Mass., but also because Lexington is where writer and editor Alice Hinkle generously helped me get my very first article published in *The Lexington Minuteman*, and where my ninth-grade English teacher made writing fun for me for the very first time and encouraged me to publish.

That teacher was/is Karen Russell, and she's still encouraging me in my professional writing career. In fact, we've reconnected as cofounders on this project and right at this very moment she's "encouraging" me to finish my introduction in the next 30 seconds so we can make our manuscript deadline for *2:25 P.M.*, and officially launch the Student Publishing Program.

The End.

Introduction from Karen Russell

Lexington High School English Teacher

Cofounder of the Student Publishing Program

At Lexington High School this year a few students and teachers swapped places for awhile; that is a student either shadowed a teacher or a teacher shadowed a student for an entire school day in an attempt to walk in each other's shoes. When we assembled in the auditorium to hear of lessons learned in this exercise, a major refrain emerged. Unless the teacher was with the student in the hours before and after school, rising before 6 a.m. to catch the bus from Boston to Lexington, for example, or going to a pre-school figure skating workout or an after school job, he or she could only grasp a truncated version of that student's experience.

So much of the quality of a student's day in school is predicated upon what happens in the context beyond the ringing of the dismissal bell at 2:25 p.m. Providing students with the venue to apply what they have learned about effective writing in school to communicate the experiences, struggles, and dreams that life outside of the classroom holds, makes a vital contribution to creating a passion for, of all things, written composition. When we listen to rather than dismiss their voices about their world outside of the classroom, then the classroom itself becomes a more dynamic place of learning.

If students know that what they write truly matters, then the writing process transcends the traditional closed circle of turning in a paper to be judged by one teacher. Instead, student writers become invested performers; their rehearsals become thoughtful revisions to their works, with an awareness of creating what is meaningful enough to contribute to a much larger audience of readers.

The submissions in *2:25 P.M.* represent 100 percent participation of sophomore students from the two classes involved in this first publication. Although the writers encompass the full spectrum of achievement in the standardized test version of academic success, the quality of each piece attests to the standard of excellence every author is able to achieve when encouraged to express a genuine point of view. Maintaining this authenticity was often even more important to us as editors than imposing grammatical corrections. Each composition is uniquely personal and original. From irreverent parody to cathartic realizations of loss, student writers demonstrate the power of creating works of poetry and prose that are written from the heart. They are a gift to the readers, a glimpse into the multifaceted prism of being a teenager in the spring of 2002.

Introduction from Scott Webber

Department Head of English Language Arts

and English Teacher

Cofounder of the Student Publishing Program

I cannot begin to tell you how excited I am about the Student Publishing Program. The project excites me both as teacher and a department head of language arts.

As a teacher working with composition writing, I have worked with students to think about audience and communication. For the most part, students have always seen me as the audience and have sought to communicate with me. Here we have an opportunity for students to publish their work to a real audience and communicate their thoughts over the Internet. This new opportunity will allow me, as well as other English teachers, to become a coach in the writing process rather than a judge of its product. Students will get feedback from a much wider audience than we could have envisioned only a short time ago.

As a department head in English language arts, I am doubly excited. First, we, in language arts, have looked for ways to bring computers to our students in meaningful and genuine ways. Doing computerized skill and drill tutorials just were not the answer. We wanted something that would truly enhance students' learning. Publishing work via the Internet provides a powerful tool for students' learning. To think that the work will be available online is one great step, but to consider collections of students' work at a particular grade level available on demand truly changes the playing field. Where once we asked students "to think of themselves as authors," we can now say, "you are authors and your work is being read across the world." Next year's sophomores will really have something by which to remember their sophomore year—beyond MCAS (Massachusetts Comprehensive Assessment System).

The second reason for my department head excitement is the authentic accountability it offers for our writing program. Everyone, those in the system, those in the community and those in the cyber community will read and judge our students' work. If the communities determine that our students' writing is lagging in a particular area, we will all know it together, and English language art teachers can make the suitable curricular changes. Further, when the entire vision is in place, and all students in grades six through twelve participate, the strengths and weaknesses of our writing program will be obvious, and our program and teachers will be accountable.

In this first decade of the new millennium, we are on the verge of charting a new course in composition that we and others will follow into the future. How exciting!

Excerpts from Student Comments on the Pilot of the Student Publishing Program

From Karen Russell's Letter to a Grant Committee
Supplementing the Student Publishing Program's Grant Proposal

Thanks to the funding provided by LHS Principal, Dr. Earnest Van Seasholes, and LHS Yearbook Advisor, Karen Mechem, we are currently working with two sophomore English classes to pilot the Student Publishing Program. These classes represent the entire spectrum of ability levels. Not only are we impressed with the exceptional pieces of poetry, fiction and essays that the students are engaged in writing for publication, we are most enthusiastic about the workshops that our writing consultant Anthony Tedesco conducted in each of our classes this week. The components are outlined within the proposal for the Student Publishing Program:

Anthony Tedesco will conduct an introductory workshop for each sophomore class. Focusing on helping students recognize themselves as worthy writers, he will introduce them to a fuller spectrum of what is considered good writing, including performance poetry videos, rap lyrics, and both conventional and unconventional pieces from historic writers, current *New Yorker* contributors, published teenage contemporaries and even samples from last year's LHS sophomores. He will also help students find and nurture their own literary voices through providing tips on the generative phase of the writing process....Finally it will debunk the myth that young people haven't lived long enough to write something of consequence, and reinforce the fact that students can be successful authors, poets and journalists right now.

We have included excerpts from the students' written responses to our request that they take a few minutes to assess the workshop. Their observations demonstrate the unprecedented level of unanimous enthusiasm expressed by both classes. The students' complete responses remain on file in our classrooms.

"This is so amazing. It makes me want to write so much more. Before I just had a feeling, a sense 'Yes, I want to be a writer when I grow up.' I have a better understanding—it's not just words on paper that are coming out of your head, it's so much feeling, so much expression of who you are and what you're feeling. You can write about anything. You can write about the simplest thing and turn it into something 'out of this world.' Now not only do I have love for writing, now I have so much passion for it. I am so excited to start. There are so many styles out there. I can't wait to taste them all."
—NICOLE TARDIFF

"...Anthony and his video showed me that you could take anything around you and turn it into personal writing, just how you feel about things, about things you want to do that may be hard to do but you want to do them anyway no matter how the odds are stacked against you."
—SHAYNE OSBOURNE

"The idea of publishing my story means to me that someone will be able to read my work. Someone out there is going to read students' work."
—DANIELA MARTINELLI

"This was helpful to me because it taught me to look at writing differently."
—MARK BRESNIHAN

"You can write anything in a poem. It doesn't have to go with each sentence. You just have to let it flow. You might not like your writing at the time, but you'll have great feedback on it."

—MARISSA COOPER

"I think the presentation was cool. It was interesting to see about all the different types of writing. It's also cool how he's telling how good it is and can be in publishing your own work…about all the different topics."
—TINA D'AMORE

"From Anthony is expressed that the simplest thing can be published and become the best. Also I realized that whatever you write can be poetry as long as you stick to it."
—TIMIKA BANKS

"…I found the session with Mr. Tedesco was extremely valuable. He seemed like a really great guy, and extremely enthusiastic about writing in general.…The most valuable thing about Mr. Tedesco's talk was the way he encouraged *our* writing. It was very effective the way he used examples from our journal entries to show how good our writing was. It gave me confidence and helped me get over my block."
—SARA DEL NIDO

"…I had forgotten, or never really realized that journal entries, little sketches and scenes, and short poems that don't tell a story all 'count' as pieces of writing…I used to think there were two different types of writing, one kind for the author himself and one kind for an audience. But, if an author really puts all of his feelings into a piece of writing for himself, I don't see how it couldn't affect an audience…"
—SAMIRA VACHANI

"…Anthony's presentation I really liked. He was very motivating and encouraging for me to write what I am really feeling. I think whatever I finally choose to write will be better…"
—SCOTT FLEISHMAN

"…His workshop was encouraging and informative about other forms of writing. It has helped also as I gained new insight about rejection and writer's block. I think student publishing may be something that I may look into further."
—RYAN TSOU

"Mr. Tedesco really made a lasting impression on me because he seemed so passionate about his own writing. He really wants to get young people published at an early age....He also had a good sense of humor and clearly loves his job as a writer. I will take all the points he brought up into consideration as I finish my creative writing piece."
—LIZ YURKEVICZ

"...I look forward to working with him on this project a little more, and think that this project is a great idea and will be a huge success this year and in the future."
—KATE GILDERSLEEVE

"...I found this quite inspiring as a writer. I also feel more comfortable with the idea of publishing my writing because my worries that no one will like my poetry have been reduced."
—ALICE WANG

"...Anthony seemed so passionate about his writing and teaching others about how to write and that everyone is capable of getting something published....After listening to Anthony and reading his packet, I realize that not everyone who writes and has things published is an amazing writer, they're just passionate about what it is they're writing."
—JAMIE BABCOCK

"Anthony offered so much inspiration. The video and packet he gave us really opened me up to all of the options available."
—SARA ARNOUDSE

Excerpts from Letters of Support for the Pilot of the Student Publishing Program

"The word is in—the Student Publishing Program is a marvelous way to motivate even the most reluctant writers. And the products are a delight to read! I wholeheartedly support this concept."
—VITO LAMURA, President, Lexington Education Association

"Your project is particularly interesting because it encourages less advanced writers to publish. The yearbook is always seeking to be inclusive in this way as well. We will see you as a 'sister publication' and hope that your writers will become our writers."
—KAREN MECHEM, LHS Yearbook Advisor

"…I never would have believed that students who in their daily content areas resist writing as a medium, flourish with their personal story under the guidance of an instructor. The stories have created the need for some to explore with a professional in bringing closure to some past hurt, anxiety or loss. In the words of one student, 'My story makes me unique.'"
—JAMES KEEFE, LHS Special Education Tutor

"I recently had the unexpected pleasure of meeting Anthony Tedesco in an English class. I was told he was our guest today as he was introduced to the class as a writer/publisher. Anthony brought with him zest and enthusiasm…I must

say it was most refreshing; students were attentive; the material was up-to-date and most of all the free style of the diverse poetic expressions empowered them to believe that they too have a story and that they can literally express it. It was just great!...Lexington High School will benefit from such a program that will enhance our traditional English Language/Literature setting."
—ANGELIA JACK, LHS Special Education Tutor

"As a teacher who is tentatively scheduled to teach four sophomore sections next year, I applaud the idea of a writing and publishing curriculum with Mr. Tedesco. Students will benefit a great deal from talking with and working with published writers and moving themselves towards their own publication....It's a great opportunity for the English department. I look forward to being a part of it."
—ELIZABETH CROWELL, LHS English Teacher

"I'm writing just to let you know that my wife and I wholeheartedly support this effort. It would be great to see a successful pilot that could eventually be incorporated into the English curriculum....In addition to possible funds available through the school budget, we are looking into whether it is possible to target a donation. It would benefit Jayme's education in the short-run, and hopefully would contribute initiating a long-term activity at LHS."
—CORVIS CATSOUPHES, Parent of a Participating LHS Student

"In an age where kids are judged more by how they do on tests than how they do with texts, *2:25 P.M.* is a breath of fresh air. As the SAT gets revised and rejiggered, this is the counter-story: the efforts by teachers of writing to document creative expression and give it a place at the table alongside those bubble tests."
—RON LIEBER, Coauthor of *Taking Time Off: Inspiring Stories of Students Who Enjoyed Successful Breaks from College and How You Can Plan Your Own,* 2nd Edition (Princeton Review) and Journalist who has written for *The Wall Street Journal, The New York Times, Fast Company, Fortune* and *Time* magazine's College Guide.

About the Cofounders

ANTHONY TEDESCO

The writer and editor leading the Student Publishing Program is Anthony Tedesco. A graduate from Lexington High School's Class of 1987, Tedesco is coauthor of the book, *Online Markets for Writers: How to Make Money by Selling Your Writing on the Internet* (Henry Holt & Co.), which has been featured in college and graduate program curricula nationwide and is now in its second printing. He's written chapters for the 1998, 1999, 2000, 2002 and 2003 editions of the book *Writer's Market* (Writer's Digest Books) and articles for such publications as *The Boston Globe, Details, Mademoiselle, The Writer* and *The Lexington Minuteman,* which published his very first article. As a guest instructor, he's taught student writers at high schools and graduate programs and, as a guest speaker, he's taught adult writers at many of the nation's largest writer conferences. Anthony also teaches and advocates for writers on radio shows such as "Connections" on National Public Radio affiliate KCLU, and television news shows such as "Money Talks," on ABC in New York and its affiliates worldwide.

KAREN RUSSELL

The teacher leading the Student Publishing Program is Karen Russell, who began teaching at Lexington High School in September of 1980. She has experience teaching English, Social Studies, and Reading and Language within the Lexington Public Schools for grades 7–12, and she has taught all levels of English within the 10–12 curriculums. While at Diamond she was the faculty liaison to artists-in-residence for the ACT Committee. Additionally, as a parent, she has served on the Fiske School Writing Committee during the 2000–2001 school year.

SCOTT WEBBER

The administrator leading the Student Publishing Program is Scott Webber, Department Head of English and Language Arts, 6–12. Scott is a teacher of over thirty years experience, serving twenty of these years as a department leader in both reading and language arts programs. He has taught at both the middle and high school levels, teaching each ability level as well as in heterogeneous settings. His conviction that effective writing emerges from the deeply seeded human urge to communicate something of him or herself to someone else guides his effort. According to him, when students know they have something to say to someone who will listen, they will create something special and worthy. Further, building these publications will provide all levels of the community with an authentic and ongoing portfolio of writing at the middle and high school levels.

2

POETRY AND PROSE FROM EVERY STUDENT IN THE CLASS

Sara Arnoudse

Privileged Secret

In the fifth grade they asked us to draw a picture
Of what we thought heaven looked like.
While all of the other little boys and girls fought over
The gold, yellow, and white pencils
To draw pictures of radiant angels
With sparkling wings and halos
Sitting upon fluffy white clouds,
I dressed the coarse construction paper
In shades of deep brown, forest green, and lake blue.

Every detail of the campground and lake flowed through the pencils
With no interruptions needed for contemplating or recollection.
RVs and tents constructed, the ranger station properly labeled
"Anger Station" where the "R" had been spray painted over—
The joke of the previous year.
At the bottom I wrote in crude cursive: Michigan (My Heaven).

When my picture was done I held it back to admire it.
Sitting in the middle of the picture was an unintended yet appropriate
beacon
Of a campfire surrounded by nine chairs.
I had never been good at drawing people so I had left them unoccupied.
The chairs may as well have been filled
For when I looked at them, I knew there was one for each of my cousins
And I knew just which chair went with whom.

When it came time to present our artwork to the class
I quickly volunteered to go first, proud of my depiction.
As I held my drawing up for the class to see,
Concealed giggles infected the classroom.
Poor Ms. Clarke thought I had misunderstood the assignment.
I hopelessly attempted to explain my masterpiece,
Not understanding why the other kids couldn't get it.
Discouraged, I hurriedly escaped back to the safety of my blue plastic chair.

The next summer as I was sitting around the campfire
With my cousins, free of worry or care and filled with bliss,
I chuckled to myself as I thought of my drawing.
Suddenly, being there, it all made sense.
Like heaven this was a place people could try to understand, picture,
But its real meaning and power was a secret,
Shared amongst those who experienced it.
A silent grin spread across my face,
Realizing what a wonderful secret we held now and forever.

Carolyn Athens

Don't Look Back

Every time she comes it's like Christmas Eve.
Without Christmas Eve there will be no excitement of Christmas.
There will be no fun or joy waiting for the presents.
Christmas Eve is a thrill and
Christmas wouldn't be the same without it.

How can a person loved so much be missed?
How can a person great with children be missed?
How can a smart person be missed?

Simple.

Chrissy Martin died by a drunk driver
In Arizona one day going to work.
Suddenly, slam, a car ran into her
And made her life instantly end.

Chrissy was my babysitter.
She was more than just a babysitter
She was like an older sister
I will never have.
She brought joy and happiness to everyone around her.

Parts of her live inside of me.
We both share the ability to put a smile on children's faces
And to see kids learn and think they're smart.

Whenever I babysit it reminds me of her.
When she would come I had a smile on my face.
And when I babysit the kids have smiles on their faces.

Live life like there is no tomorrow
And cherish everything you do.
Don't look back, never look back.

Although she is gone physically, she is not gone mentally.
She lives in my heart, mind, and soul.
I know I will see her one day when I take my trip up to Heaven.

There is no more Christmas Eve.

Jamie Babcock

Why Are You So Good To Me?

Wandering down the lonely halls
no sense of purpose or meaning
A spirited voice shouts and calls
The day is transformed and all is well
Please take me away from this icy hell
Let's retreat to our own world frozen in time
protected from hate and materialism
Help me find myself in you.

Your words lift me up, wash away my fears
A gentle touch calms my rushing emotions
merely your presence can make a bad day good
a good day better.

I dream that I can someday change your life in the ways that you have mine
A kind heart filled with love
A willing soul and a lending ear
two kindred spirits meant for one another
my guardian angel.

Why are you so good to me?
Why do you always say the right words to dry my tears?
You make me laugh
You ease my pain
Why can you agree with me and share your feelings without a word
You've changed me in so many ways, for better.

I wish I could put into words all that you mean to me
You are my best friend, my other half
My hope is that you are able to realize that
When you're not around anymore, I know that through you I will
have gained
the strength to be
on my own.

You are my protector and mentor
Why are you so good to me?
Am I the same to you?

Do I lead you on journeys new and pick you up when you stumble?
If I can mean one pinch of what you mean to me I will be satisfied.

Your kindness and wisdom have made me eternally grateful
Without you I am nothing.

Timika Banks

Blood Is Thicker Than Water

*The proverb "Blood is thicker than water" means
no matter what happens, family will be there
when friends are not.*

I am pregnant at fifteen years old
and I didn't know how to tell my mother.
I was at school one day and someone
called and told my mother that I was pregnant.
When I went home that day I took a nap.
My mother woke me up and said
someone called and told me that you're pregnant,
and she wanted to know if it was true.
I said I didn't know.
Later she said that she thought
I could come to her
and that she wouldn't have to hear it
from someone else.

She took me to the clinic
and, after 101 questions,
I took the pregnancy test.
They told me I was pregnant.
My mother stayed with me and
said she would support me
in any decision I made.
I don't believe in abortion

because that is killing a human being.
So I decided to have the baby.

My mother will share custody of the baby
with me and help me. My friends
thought it was cute that I was pregnant,
but my mother stepped in and supported me.
Family stays with you
through rough times,
even if they don't agree
with your decision.

Now time has passed and I'm six months
into my pregnancy. School's become different.
I'm one out of hundreds of kids pregnant.
Many kids just stare at me,
wondering, is she really pregnant,
while others ask me.

No one has made me feel uncomfortable.
But there are many times I sit back
and just want to cry 'cause
I'm having a baby and
I don't know what to expect
for trouble in life with the baby.
But I do know I'll be there to do my best
with the help of my family and the baby's father.

Since January, when I first felt my baby move,
I knew that this was no joke, and even now
I lay down at night, twisting and turning
'cause the baby is kicking me.
It's hard trying to sleep with something
moving around in your stomach.

I must say, no one can understand my situation
until they live it as a teenager.
But I still believe that having this baby
is the right thing to do.

Zander Bauman

Big Debut

My name is Kent Wallace, and I am an amateur filmmaker. All my life I've loved movies, going entire weeks where the only time I left my house was to get some more tapes out of Blockbuster. And all my life I've been thinking up my own, from the monster movies I made with my little brother as a kid to the teen angst movies I made as a preteen. All my life I've been waiting for this moment, the moment that is about to come. Because now, after all these years of pondering, I'm ready. I am finally capable enough, old enough, and mature enough to do it. I am ready to make my big debut. But I can't just debut with anything. A debut's gotta be big. Many filmmakers never make a movie better than their first one. Case in point: Mel Brooks hit his peak with *The Producers*, his first time as writer and director. Another example: while highly debatable, I find that Kevin Smith's *Clerks* is the best of his New Jersey trilogy, although all of the five have very strong supporters. A strong debut is what makes you.

"You're going to remake *The Godfather*?" asked Mark.

"It's not a remake," I said. "It's a reenvisioning."

"That's just a fancy way of saying a remake," said Mark.

"No," I said, "because in a reenvisioning you take a movie and play it up in a completely different way. It's not a redone version of the original, it's a completely different movie with a similar premise."

"Oh, so like Tim Burton's *Planet of the Apes*?"

"Yes," I said, "except without the suck."

"It's *The Godfather*!" said Mark. "The greatest movie ever made! How do you think you can top that?"

"I agree that it has many good aspects, but any movie has room for improvement."

"Ok," said Mark, "tell me how you would improve *The Godfather*."

"Well," I said, leaning back in my chair, "I have tons of ideas. Like, for instance, instead of Michael hiding in Sicily, he should go to the Middle East, so we can get that whole Osama bin Laden angle in there. You know, play towards the modern crowd?"

"That's the stupidest thing I've ever heard," said Mark.

"Also," I said, "we can beef up Kay's part to give her a whole side story while Michael's in the Middle East, something about her becoming a stripper. And we need far more sex scenes."

"That totally cheapens the whole concept!"

"No," I said, "it's artistic."

"So what do you want me to do?" Mark asked.

"To be in it, of course," I said.

"Well who could I be?" he asked. "I'm not Italian, I'm not good-looking, and I'm not even any good at acting. The only reason I'm ever in any of these movies is 'cause you ask me."

"I got it!" I said. "Well, who's not Italian in the movie? Tom Hagen. It'd be a perfect part for you."

"Tom Hagen? As in the part Robert Duvall played? How do you expect me to play a part once done by Robert Duvall?"

"It's a reenvisioning," I explained. "It'll be like a completely different part. You'll hardly even recognize the character Robert Duvall played. So are you in?"

"This is the dumbest project I've ever heard of," Mark said.

"So you're in?" I asked.

"Well, yeah," he said. "It's not like I've got anything better to do."

As my best friend, I needed Mark on the project to give me the go-ahead, to tell me that it was as viable a project as it appeared in my mind. If Mark wasn't in, then there'd be no point in me attempting it. Sure, I could find better actors than Mark, but the moral support he gave me was unmatched. So with the ok by Mark, I began the script. I watched the beginning of the movie again, and still wasn't sure how I wanted the movie to begin. So I reread the first part of the book. The book starts a little before the movie, showing all the people who go to Don Corleone for help before Connie's wedding. So I figured I'd beat that by starting even earlier chronologically. Once I got the beginning set, I easily got the first two scenes written. With a beginning set, I knew the rest of it would write itself, so I immediately went to work on casting.

You can't have a movie without a lead. I mean, sure, there are lots of ensemble movies out there, which sometimes work and sometimes don't. And even in those kinda movies characters stick out. Even in *Pulp Fiction* you can still call John Travolta the lead. So that was where I wanted to start. Once I had a lead, everyone else would fall into place. It's like in Hollywood. They spend years searching for a lead, but they all come in packs. You take one guy you also get a director, a lead actress, a camera man, and a best boy. You take another actor you get a supporting actress, a writer, and a casting agency. You take a third guy you get him as director, his brother as screenwriter, and a trained monkey to make a cameo in the movie. It's all very political. So I went to work, until I found the perfect guy to play my Michael.

"Hola Señor Daniel!" said Jorge.

"Jorge, it's Kent now, not Dan." I said.

"Señor Daniel, ¿qué puedo hacer para ti?"

"Well, you see Jorge, I'm making a movie, and I want you to be the lead. You're perfect for the role. It's a guy who wanted to do it his way, but got caught up in family business. And there's a salsa dance scene that'd be perfect for you."

"No hablo ninguna palabra de inglés."

"You're in? Great!"

With Michael cast, I knew the rest of the guy parts could be filled easily. But getting some of the girl spots filled, that could be a bit trickier. Now most of the girls in my crew wouldn't be so hard to lure over, always ready at the promise of possible stardom, a chance to show off their dramatic ability, and a couple of bucks for being in it (compared to what they pay in Hollywood....or Newton for that matter, it's nothing. Seriously, I pay like $5). However, Gloria wasn't like most of the girls in my crew. Namely because she wasn't in my crew, and yet I knew I could find no one else for the part of Apollonia that would satisfy me. It had to be her.

"This isn't going to be like your last movie, is it?" asked Gloria.

"No, that movie had a different purpose. This one will be more tuned down towards the masses."

"It didn't make any sense Dan," she said.

"It's Kent now, Gloria, and it did make sense. You just have to be able to see it at its artistic level."

"All I know is that I was sitting on a flower pot with a snake between my teeth while Mark read off a list of the elements."

"You were symbolizing Eve, with the snake already there, yet at the same time you were also the Tree of Life, so though you fell you are still what life is, and the elements represented what life is made of on a more basic level, the inorganic components."

"That's the biggest load of bullshit I've ever heard."

"Listen," I said, "you just stick to acting. It's my job to explain it, you just go into it."

"So I read the first part of your screenplay. I'm not in it."

"You don't appear towards later, but you definitely play a crucial role."

"Dan..." she said.

"What?"

"This isn't just some dumb attempt to win me back, is it?"

"Of course not," I said. "We broke up months ago. I've accepted it, I've moved on. I want you in this for two reasons: as an actress and a friend. We're all in this together Gloria. Anyway, we start shooting tomorrow at noon. Meet in Mark's backyard at 11:30. You probably won't be in the scene, but be there so we can all talk about the project anyway, ok?"

"Ok Dan," she said. "But do me a favor, ok?"

"What?" I said.

"Stop calling yourself Kent. The name doesn't fit you."

On my way out, I stopped and turned to say one more thing. "Oh, by the way. You will be nude throughout the entire movie."

EXT Mark's House 11:30 AM Shooting Day

"Where do you want me to film it from?" asked Ian.

"That spot's good, just keep it steady," I said.

"All right," said Ian. "*The Next Godfather* take 1!"

And like that, my life as a filmmaker had begun.

Any Body

Turning Points

1.

The day was cold and windy and it was a Friday in November. I didn't have to go to school because my grandmother died and it was the morning of her funeral. The morning was rushed because we were trying to get an early start. My 17 year-old sister was busy getting dressed; it always takes her longer. Finally, my mom, my sister and I got into the car. The drive was usually five to ten minutes, but it took a little longer because of the traffic.

We drove from the South End of Boston to Roxbury where my father lived. The house is a triple-decker, painted brown with a small lawn in front. There's a pathway that goes next to the house, and that's how we always go in. I remember when we pulled up to his house, parked on the street, and used the front door. We usually don't go that way. My little brother, who lives with my father, opened the door to let us in. He is two years old and was dressed in a tuxedo. I never saw him dressed like that.

When the door opened, I smelled candles. They smelled like roses. You know how candles have that burning smell? That was mixed with the rose smell. The living room was a lot cleaner than it used to be. The kitchen connects to the living room, and on the kitchen table was a full face picture of my grandmother with her glasses on. There was one of those rose smelling candles on each side and red flowers were in front of the picture.

My step-sister, who is 12, came up to me and said "Hi." My little brother, who came to the door, was just jumping around on me, happy to see me. Other family members came into the house and everybody hugged.

We all went outside because the limousines were there. Some family members came late, and we had to figure out what limo to put them in. There were three limos, so some people had to drive themselves over to the church. I got into the limo with my father, uncle and two younger brothers. We left his house and turning the corner saw a fire at a house which caused the street to be blocked off by police officers. We had to find another way to get out. We turned around and drove to the church for the funeral.

The church was old-fashioned, dark brown, and wooden with two sets of stairs in front. The first set went to a platform, and the other set led up to dark brown doors that were open. We got out of the car and went inside the church.

My father walked ahead of us by himself. The pastor was already in the church, and male ushers were the only ones in the church besides my grandmother's open casket. I couldn't really see her from the back of the church. I could only see my father's back getting smaller as he got further away. I was trying to follow him, but some other family members got ahead of me. There were three aisles in the church, and he was walking away from the casket down a side aisle. I saw him crying and holding his hands up to his face. He walked into a back room, and my mom told me to go see what's wrong with him. I went into the back room. He turned and hugged me and cried on my shoulder. I never saw him cry before and I was surprised. I remember feeling really bad for him because he loved her really well. I started to cry too because I felt the same pain he felt. The more I watched him cry the more I did. It was the most memorable moment of my life.

2.

I felt like I messed up most of my life and I never do anything right. It happened again today. I came back to the resource room and I've been upset all day. I had been okay since English class and then I came back to get construction paper, and the teacher asked me to call my father. Then I felt my stomach drop like a bomb from a plane. I remember the words of my father crying, "You're going to get it when you get home." Yet this isn't where the story begins.

It was January after Christmas break and I was happy to come back. More of the things I do in school and "out of school" in the same day. I was happy to see all my friends. I was happy to get out the crib. I was happy to hear all of the kids jabbering in the hallway of school about how great their vacation was. I remember my teacher talking about an after school studying thing for a stupid test in the state that all tenth graders had to take. I thought this was an opportunity to use an excuse to cover up the detentions I had recently got before the vacation. So I had told my father that day when I got home about it and asked him if I could go. He told me to tell my teacher to call him to confirm that it was true since I had built a reputation in the past for being deceitful. Yet that didn't stop me from doing it anyway. I really didn't care at that point in time. I just didn't want to set off his anger. My father is the type of person that's very easily angered. So it was set. I would be free after school for four months to do whatever I pleased. I went to the detentions, but after those were done I had to have something to do. Should I actually go to the studies or chill with friends. Surely there was something I could do. So I did what naturally came to my mind which was hang with my friends. So I figured out what to do with my friends which was the only thing I could think of—smoke.

Smoking was the only thing in the world that would take away the pain that wasn't displayed to the face of anyone else. It gave me the edge that I needed to get through the rest of my day. I knew I was depressed, but I didn't want to show it.

The first time I smoked, I feared that other people would find out I had never tried it before, and I would be the laughingstock of the school again. So I played like I had done it, just to do it. I hadn't wanted to try it for many years, but there was something in the back of my head that told me just to try it once to see if it will do something for me.

I remember looking at the long narrow brown paper with the green filling as it came out the pocket of my friend's red jacket. I was saying to myself, "I'm actually doing this." There were many people there so it took a while before it got to me. So when it got to me I was anxious. So I quickly held it up and I lit it. I sucked in the smelly smoke, and it quickly went down my throat and burned me. So I did what naturally came to thought which was to cough. Everybody stared and laughed as I took another try at it. This time it didn't burn as much. So I was able to inhale. It was the first time that I felt successful at anything. I was happy as the smoke took effect. I was blazed for the first time ever.

I never thought doing this would ever lead to the kind of life that I live now. For a while nothing happened to me. I never got caught, and I felt I was happier with myself. So I did what I had to do continually for the next year. Then summer came, so I was away from friends and smoking for two and a half months. Then school started again and I was definitely back to old habits. But this time even more so than last year. I was down to smoking every day as opposed to maybe twice a week. It continued until one day me and two of my smoking buddies got caught by the police. My two buddies were expelled, but the only reason I didn't get into trouble was I wasn't necessarily involved. So then again I messed up. I had quit for awhile, but that didn't stop me from starting back up. So I smoked and smoked and smoked.

Now, back to where I had left you hanging. My father found out that what had started from a simple lie blew up to a giant consequence. I felt too scared to go home, so I did the first thing that came to my mind which was to run away. There was too much fear in my mind and chest building up to even think about going home.

So I went to a friend's house to crash. We hung around at his house for awhile, then we did the only thing that came to mind, which was to smoke. As soon as I inhaled the scrawny little thing, it instantly took every emotion that I had on my mind away. I was fearless for about two hours and it felt great. Then I realized that what I was doing was the wrong way to approach my problems.

I dialed my grandmother up on the phone. The fear kept building up under my skin like a volcano ready to erupt. Finally, she picked up the phone and said "Hello." She told me that everybody was so scared about what happened to me. I could hear the sigh of relief in her voice. Then she told my mother and father that I was okay. Later on they called me and yelled every bit of anger they had into me.

It was worth it to come back. Yet I knew nothing would be the same. There would be a lot of pressure on me to be better. All my trust from my parents would mean nothing to them. School would have to change. Life would have to be better. Smoking would have to stop. But I would not see the last of it.

Mark Bresnihan

Money

I enjoy getting paid from my job.
It may sound stupid

but having money—
green, weightless, small, thin—

makes some things
enjoyable.

Like if I'm going out with my friends
and we want to go do something

I will have money. Money
buys you everything.

Brad Buchinski

Driving

1.

I like going driving now.
But I can remember my first time out
when I hit a tree.
It's funny now
but it was scary then.

2.

Now I can't get enough driving.
Like last night when I drove to my cousins.
I got seated in the Volvo Cross Country.
I'm used to the car.
I was excited.
I would be driving on Route 2 West
which is like a small highway…for me anyway.
It was a good drive.
I just came close to one accident this time
on the hard winding roads of Bolton.

Jayme Catsouphes

As Is

From a not completely
Forgotten corner
You seduce me
I'll do as you order

But it goes

Day slides into day
And though I try
I can't make my love for you stay
And I ask myself why

You always have to fight
Why I can't see you tonight
Why you can't
Accept me as is

I call at two
As you'd want me to
It's late
Feelings of hate brew

So I go

Next day
"You don't love me"

That's what you say
And I can't see why

You always have to fight
Why I can't just see you tonight
Why you can't
Accept me as is

You say
I avoid confrontation
You say
You create confrontation
I say
You create stress and tension

There's a difference

How dare you be so hypocritical
Your words hit me
Like a hammer would tickle
Have you no pity

I want to scream

I'm sick of reading
Your hidden messages
Your life is a play
People are your stages

How How How

How dare you be so hypocritical
Your words hit me
Like a hammer would tickle
Have you no pity

You think you're so much better

Saima Chaudry

Murmurs

So soft the sound of silence
So quiet
Standing under the monstrous gleam of the moonlight
I stood there on the outside looking in
Stood as the mist's mysterious fog enveloped me
Like the dark swallowing the light
A burnt out candle
Flickering in my own grief-stricken hallway
The door was open
But I knew that it wasn't an invitation waiting for me
I was the cold draft on a dark winter's night
While they were the seething fire
Never knowing the damage they caused
From the inside out
I looked down upon puddles of tears
Now the mirror of my sorrow
My reflection seeing through the shell to the soul
The soft whispers of the wind
Murmuring the voices cradled in my head
From the outside looking in
I saw more than there was to be seen
I saw what they couldn't see.
The light that they were hiding from.

Gillian Conklin

Volunteering At Winchester Hospital

I am in Winchester Hospital.
I have been volunteering for
two years this summer.
I'm here every Saturday
from 12 p.m. to 3 p.m.
Some things I do:
discharge people,
bring specimens to the lab,
bring patients to different places,
and other errands.

I do this
for community service. But
I enjoy helping out people who are sick
because I care about them.
I have always wanted to be a nurse.
These hours will be good for college.

Not only do I enjoy helping out
but also meeting other volunteers.
We have to wear red shirts
to distinguish between
those who are volunteers
and those who aren't.

Marissa Cooper

Daeja

1.

Amazing grace how sweet the sound
Of her little voice that sounds so loud.
I have a niece; she is very special to me.
She brings me love and joy. She means everything to me.
When I'm down, she brings me up.
When she cries, I wipe the tears from her eyes
She doesn't like to see me sad
So she always does something to make me laugh.

On January 17, 2000, a baby girl was born.
She was the quietest little thing that you ever did see.
As I watch her color come in.
Looking through that window while the nurse checks her up.
Seeing her squirming around on the table
Like a caterpillar searching for food.
Seeing her made everything right.
It was like being in a world where nothing goes wrong
But you always have to stop and think that no one is innocent for long.

I always wanted a little sister but the day never came.
So when my brother told me I was going to be an Auntie,
I was so happy, that my face said a thousand words.

He told me it was going to be a girl
I thought…Here's my little sister!
Then waiting for those long impatient nine months to come.
Waiting   Thinking   Waiting
Thinking in my head, what is she going to look like?
What is she going to sound like?
How will she cry?
Those were some killer months.
Till that day came and she was here!

I remember the first time I was holding her.
Smelling so fresh and sweet like a little kid being in a candy store!
When I was holding her I never wanted to let go.
Looking at this precious gift with a purpose and plan.
Was something special to me!

Now she is two, a bundle of joy.
A handful she is.
She thinks she is grown but little does she know.
She wants to do everything and anything.
She looks up to me so I have to watch my action.
I have to think twice before I do.
I would do anything for her.
I love her to death.

2.

I am on the bus
on a Monday morning.
Wondering
how my day is
going to go.
Looking
out of the window.
Seeing
cars go by

on the highway.
Then
I stop.

Looking around the bus,
everyone seems so
dead,
tired
and
weary
from the
weekend.

Just thinking about
school is like drowning
in a pool.

Feel that
this
is going to be
a long week.

Erica Crowe

Loss

The wind blowing left to right
Sun shining for a cause unknown
Tears flowing like rivers of sadness
Thoughts of prayers, wishing to join
Flashes of color, yellow, red,
purple…to black
Nighted color black, consuming cotton,
nylon and polyester
Why this? Why now?
What are we learning?
Where is the lesson?

Time passing, reversing never
if only…if only
Pictures the only memory left
How can it be?
Colored pigment on concentrated
pressed paper, all that is left

Vaulted ceilings, Row after row
Perpendicular wood hanging
What is the meaning?
Not so sure anymore
Drops on the paper tissue
Try to stay strong,
Must stay strong

Feelings of sorrow consume the soul
How affected, How afraid
Never experienced such sorrow

Petals now beginning to wilt
Crumble and fall to the ground
Renew
Cold cement block of death
Such meaning
Why?

Tina D'Amore

Martial Arts

Seven years ago something came into my life
that changed my perspective on life
and how to react to things. This something was
the study of Martial Arts. With Martial Arts
I learned how to control and limit my anger.
It made me an overall different person.

A couple of months ago,
there was a party I was going to
that my best friend, Sara, was not.
The reason was that she was spending
the night with her boyfriend
because that party happened to be
on the same day as their anniversary.
This brought up bad and mean thoughts
from some of her closest friends
including me. Since she wasn't at the party,
my other good friends, Jess, Danielle, and me,
decided to discuss the situation.
After, the three of us felt bad talking about her
without her there, so we thought we should
tell her how we felt. Me, being her closest friend,
thought I should be the one to tell her.
The next morning I called her and told her
everything the three of us had talked about.
She immediately got mad and started

yelling about talking behind her back.
This is what helped me really learn
what the study of Martial Arts did for me.

The situation with Sara and me got
even worse than verbal. One day
she came to my locker and started yelling at me.
Before we even started yelling, she pushed me.
Now with all the anger I had built up inside,
I wanted to push her back
and cream her in the face with my fist.
But what I realized by studying Martial Arts
is that I had learned to use my self-control
and not push her or hit her in the face.

Hitting back and starting something
isn't the right way to handle things.
Walking away and stopping a fight waiting to happen
helped show me something I had inside of me
that I could never even know about
if it weren't for Sara and our fight.
I thank Sara for showing me
this controlled and good part of myself.
I wouldn't be the same unique person I am today,
and I'm grateful for every trait I hold now.

Sara DelNido

Gone

"The Sara we used to know is gone."

Gone.
I'm gone
My mom says so.
At this time last year, I was going out with friends
Picking the next day's outfit
Trying to devise a way to get myself to the senior prom.

Now I'm crying
Crying crying
Like I do every day
In bed, late at night, when no one can see me
Like I am inside, every second of every day
Internal bleeding
No one sees it.

Why have I put on such a mask?
Heavy mask of makeup that acts as a shield to hold in my
feelings
Hasn't failed me yet.
Why have I become like this?
Crying crying like a baby
The tears don't do anything
Useless

Duh, I knew that
Yet now I sit on my bed and listen to the wind blazing outside
Like a whirlwind of insanity
Uncontainable
Unrestrainable
Hearing the taunting music in my head
Discordant and sad
Twisting my mind until all I hear is a scream
Which I cannot utter

Enjoying the darkness
Thick black
Shutting out life
And numbing me to myself.
Still crying.
Hotness dripping like bitter honey onto my once pure cheeks
A face that knew no true sadness.

I used to want to do things
Succeed, laugh, work, make myself beautiful
Now why do I want to do none of those things?
Why? Why? Why? Why?
Where am I?
Who am I?
Where is Sara?

How did she go away?
How can I find her and bring her back?
It's like that line from Linkin Park
"If I'm killed by the questions like a cancer,
Then I'll be buried in the silence of the answer by myself."

Myself
I don't know who that is
Even the word sounds strange
I've forgotten the definition, where's a dictionary?

Last year I guess it was someone
Content with herself
Satisfied
Happy

So why is it that I hate life now?
Why why.
I can feel my personality slipping away
Every day
A little more sand through my fingers
A little more Sara is gone.
And when I look in the mirror
I see all the things that I never wanted to be.

Aram Demirjian

Glamour: An American In Paris

Inspired by George Gershwin's An American in Paris

The mist of early morning Paris was just beginning to clear as I walked from my hotel. Mere minutes had passed since sunrise, and the city was already beginning to come alive. It had been a rainy night, and the damp cobblestones beneath the smooth soles of my shoes were still slick. A taxicab with a rather energetic driver sped by honking its horn, announcing to the masses that it was morning and that it was time to wake up and get to work. I considered calling one of those taxis to drive me to my destination, but I realized that I had no destination, and it was much more pleasurable to walk.

As I neared an area of shops, the level of activity began to pick up. The sun was now upon us in all of its glamour, erasing the gloomy, stormy remnants of the night before. I decided to sit down at a café for my breakfast. As I drank my café au lait and devoured my crusty French bread, I observed the hustle and bustle of passersby. There was one lone police officer directing traffic, desperately trying to make sense of it all. This brought me thoughts of America and the similar organized chaos I observed every morning.

At this point, Luxembourg Gardens seemed to be a suitable destination. So, I took my walking stick in hand and made my way through the lively streets of Paris. My surroundings tickled my senses as I walked. The smells of freshly baked bread and crepes wafted into my nose, and the performers on the side-walks filled the air with jubilant music. As I walked, street vendors attempted to sell me everything from fine jewelry to used books to week-old newspapers. They were quite relentless. As they continued to talk, it became harder and harder to break free of their sales pitch. The street performers stood out most of all. Human statues were the most popular, but there were also some sword swallowers and even a fire breather. Just in front of the gate to the Gardens, I bumped into a mime. I suppose I must have somehow become trapped in his invisible box. After taking some trouble to escape, I bid the mime good day and entered the Gardens. There was a gazebo there in which an orchestra was playing. I made my way over to a bench by the fountains, and I sat to enjoy the warm, bright midday sun. There were what appeared to be millions of pigeons all over. They almost outnumbered the multitude of gorgeous flowers that were about the whole garden. There were children playing all about; however, right then they seemed to be distracted by a candy salesman who had wandered by. I lay my head back. I did not know whether I was asleep or awake, whether this was a dream or a reality. Either way, I did not favor the idea of spending my entire stay in Paris sitting on a bench pondering. The Eiffel Tower dominated the horizon to the south, and I was determined to get there as quickly as I could.

I went there by taxi. To this day I think my driver was the same crazy man who was driving the taxi I saw that morning, for throughout the entire wild cab-ride, I feared we were going to run ourselves off the rode. I arrived safely, however. As the elevator in which I rode climbed up the Tower, and the world below began getting smaller, I felt a strange feeling welling up inside of me. When I reached the top, and looked out at the city, I finally realized the true beauty of Paris. I felt like it was just the city and me flying over it, no distractions, nobody else; perfectly serene and peaceful. But, in Paris, one can never be without distractions for too long. This time it was the ding of my pocket watch. I had heard about a large ball that was being held that night, and having not been invited, I felt it was only suitable to invite myself. Who could deny a man of that on his first night in Paris? I began to cross the gravel underneath the Tower with the intent of catching a trolley back to my hotel.

And then I saw her.

She had red hair and was wearing a designer dress. She had on one of those hats with an incredibly large round brim, and she had her sunglasses lowered onto her nose. She was even more radiant than the sun that illuminated her. I considered asking her to accompany me to the ball that I was going to attend. But she was French; she would not want anything to do with a classless American such as myself. I cannot remember clearly, but I must have looked away for a moment because when I looked again, she was gone with the afternoon breeze. I consoled myself by remembering that beautiful women were not uncommon in Paris, but in my heart I was still disappointed. My disappointment was temporarily smothered, however, because with or without the red-haired lady, I had a ball to get ready for, and the late-afternoon sun was beginning to set. Night slowly crept upon the city as I made my way back to the hotel. The liveliness of the morning once more appeared as people began to head home at the end of the day. My day, however, was just beginning. I quickly stopped into my room to freshen up and put on my tuxedo; then I was right back out the door. A car and chauffeur were already waiting for me. I sat down in the leather interior of the car and entered Paris at night.

Lights were already flashing on, and my excitement continued to grow as each light turned on. The red lights on the Eiffel Tower were blazing like fireworks, standing out against the backdrop of dark, black sky. Anything illuminated seemed remarkably larger at night than it did during the day. I arrived at the hall where the ball was taking place; I could already hear the band playing inside. There were many well-dressed men and women like myself who were just arriving. Inside the hall, for the first time I came to the realization that I was crashing this party. I was not quite sure what to do at that point. I was not in my element at all, with the huge glass chandeliers and marble floors and free wine that would normally have cost me one of my limbs. Also, I was the only one without a dance partner.

And then she was there again.

She had removed the hat and sunglasses and was wearing a different dress, but she was still unmistakably the jaw-dropping red-haired beauty that I encountered earlier in the day. The color of her dress matched her hair. This time, I promised myself I would not let her disappear. I approached her, and in the little French that I knew, I said hello. I received an equally friendly greeting from her. Then came that awkward silence. Everybody has felt it. Either due to a language barrier or insecurity around a person to whom you are attracted, in this case both, neither person wants to make the first move. I finally, in broken French, mustered up the courage to ask her to dance.

The band broke into swing, and we danced the night away. It was wonderful. We twirled, whirled, and dipped across the dance floor for hours. Just when it seemed that the night could not get anymore glamorous, the clock struck midnight. She told me she had to leave. I never had the heart to ask why, I was too upset. I escorted her out to her car, kissed her hand, and she was off. I never saw my red-haired Cinderella again. I went to sit down on a bench outside the hall with my head hung low. I felt very much like feeling sorry for myself. I was almost prepared to leave and go back to the hotel, but then I remembered where I was. I stopped wallowing in self pity long enough to realize that the sights, the sounds, and the smells were still there, I had only forgotten to notice them. I made one more promise there and then, that I would never forget to notice them again. I picked myself up, loosened my collar, and began to walk away from the ball, and towards the lights of the city. I had no destination. All I knew was that somewhere in this vast city, there was another party even better than this one, another Cinderella was out there, and something incredible was just waiting to happen. Would I find it that night? Perhaps, perhaps not. But the night is young for a man like me, an American in Paris.

John-Michael Denney

Henry

A long time ago there was a boy named Michael who owned two cats, Boe and Henry. The cats shared a litter box that was a gateway to hell. Now, if you've ever been there, hell is not such a bad place. If you play your cards right, you can go to the air-conditioned section. Sure there are some people who are in constant agony, but those are just the Catholics (they have to have it their way). Satan is evil, true, Satan is the devil, true, Satan is out to get as many souls as he can, false. Satan just wants to practice his archery, chill with his minions, and have an occasional perfect Manhattan. To do this, however, Satan has to possess a mortal being and transcend to the human plane of existence.

This isn't so bad for the "damned"; they usually live and get their souls back. Sometimes Satan makes mistakes, grave errors of epic proportions, when he is on the human plane. Remember "Cheese Whiz with Bacon?"

Our story takes place during the time of Satan's 64869th error, Henry. Henry was a cat who would've made his ancestors proud. Henry hunted people. He stalked small prey like mice and birds, but only when he couldn't find a person to hunt. He also stalked little kids through the woods. He even hunted his owner Mike, who is not exactly a small man. Henry attacked Mike so often that it drove him to take drastic actions. One day, when Henry was sneaking up on what he thought was a sleeping Mike, Mike pulled out a super soaker, named Death, that made hoses look like water fountains. The spray knocked Henry out of the room and almost down the stairs. After that, Mike didn't have any more problems with Henry. One day, when Mike went upstairs to feed the cats, he heard a voice.

"Pssst, buddy."

Mike thought to himself, "Whoa, drank too much Surge." He kept on walking. The voice came up again.

"Pssst, buddy, yeah you."

Mike turned to the litter box, "That better not be you."

The litter box suddenly grew a face and smiled at Mike, "You, uh, wanna buy a limb?"

Mike put his can of Surge down and looked at the litter box as it pushed an arm out of the kitty litter.

"No, I don't want to buy a limb, where the hell did you get that?"

"Hell," the litter box responded.

"Oh," Mike turned and began to walk away. As he looked back, the litter box was trying to sell a finger to one of Mike's slippers. "Huh," Mike thought, "my litter box is a gateway to hell. I'm hungry."

Mike was still thinking about how hungry he was as Henry passed him whilst on his way to the litter box. Henry, not being afraid of anything except the Super-Soaker named Death, walked right into the talking litter box and proceeded to do his business. Henry got up a couple of minutes later, possessed by Satan, and seemingly normal. However all was not normal. Besides having his soul replaced with Satan, Henry could walk upright, and his vocal cords were mutating so that he could speak the tongues of man.

"Fele foedissimo, quid hades?"(What the hell, I'm a freakin' cat?) Mike walked by muttering to himself, "The cat isn't walking upright, and it certainly isn't talking."

Satan looked around. "Sum feles, in albo dormo, in suburbe." (I'm a cat, in a white house, in suburbia.) Great, just freakin' great. I should better start speaking English." He turned to the litter box, "I don't suppose this is your doing."

"No, of course not." The litter box responded. "By the way, can I interest you in some of my merchandise?"

"No you cheating litter bastard," Satan said, "I own those limbs. Wait, is that my nose? You took that cat's nose?" Satan leaped at the litter box. "Give me that back."

After smacking up the litter box a bit, Satan proceeded to travel around his new house and neighborhood. He scoped out the area, looking for someone or something else to possess. He had little luck. Most of Mike's neighbors were on vacation, or if they were there, they ran when they saw a cat walking on two feet chanting incomprehensible Latin phrases.

After two days of unsuccessful attempts to change bodies, Satan realized that he had one rather ignorant, easy target right under his fingertips. A docile, stupid, and powerful creature he could take over—Boe the cat!

Satan had one problem, which was that Mike avidly defended Boe when he saw him under attack by Henry. So Satan searched deep into the bowels of hell for a fighting genius whose spirit he could use to battle Mike.

Days later, after intense meditation, Satan was finally ready to face Mike in open combat. Imbued with the spirit of Napoleon, the undefeatable French general, Henry would be invincible. Mike would stand no chance against the elemental force that is Napoleon.

As Mike started to walk down the stairs, Satan charged up to meet him and began to morph. Mike's face changed from surprise, to fear, back to surprise, then to humor, then to shock as his cat morphed from a foot-tall cat, to a four foot-tall man.

"Ah ha ha ha," Satan boomed, well, boomed as much as a little man can, and said, "What are you going to do now, mortal?"

Mike kicked Napoleon down the stairs.

The little fat man rolled and rolled, until he hit the bottom step and broke his neck.

Satan's soul immediately flew out of Napoleon, into the litter box, and back to hell. Whether they were directly affected or not, in all the world, nobody's life was ever the same since the Satan incident.

Mike had to explain to his family why Henry was gone, and why there was a dead Napoleon in their living room. Mike's family decided to stuff and mount Napoleon. He is currently under bid on Ebay for four dollars.

Satan returned to the underworld without accomplishing any of his original goals. He now lies in waiting until he gets another chance to possess a soul.

The spirit of Henry is missing. Rumor has it he possessed a lamp; the lamp was not available for questioning.

Ebag Dlonra

Ebullient Doppelganger

Traversing the street
                                        Under a neon orange sky,
                    There seems to be someone else there.
I think we'd like to meet,
                                        But maybe that's just a lie.
                    Cuz he gives one heluva stare.
I know I've seen him around,
                                        He seems familiar,
                    Yet I can't quite figure it out.
He moves by without a sound
                                        And it really is peculiar,
                    That I haven't seen him about.
As I continue on my way,
                                        I stop by a mirror
                    And then it hits me strong
The astonishment of my day,
                                        To my sudden stupor,
                    He was me all along.

Tyler Edell

The Shark, The Catcher, And Spiderman

I had never accomplished something of this magnitude. I was chosen as the catcher for the 16-year-old Goodwill Series team. I was on my way to Australia to play against the top Australian baseball teams in my age group. Granted, I expected the trip to be different, but I had no clue what was in store for me.

The day is the thirteenth of December. This is my first trip out of the state in my whole life. Needless to say, I almost break out crying every time I hear screaming or I think that I lost my ticket at the airport. It makes me feel really idiotic, considering that my argument to keep my mom from coming was that "I can take care of myself, mom, I'm 16 for God's sake!"

I can't even stand up for myself when a toddler decides to punch me in the butt when I'm waiting in line to check in. I guess that explains why Diego and I immediately don't like each other.

The first thing he says to me is, "Yo, you Mark? You look pretty gay with that hat. *Pff* Loser."

"Shut the hell up, jerk."

"'Scuse me? You sound like you're trying to start a little scuffle here. Is that it, bitch? You wanna fight?"

"No, man, forget it."

And with that terrifyingly pitiful attempt at proving my manhood, I sit down. Shortly after, three more kids show up, each welcomed by Diego's observation about how "gay" they each look. As it turns out, this is the team's core—the catcher, me, an amazing pitcher, Mike "Maverick" Sinadry, the shortstop, Diego "Spiderman" Rivera, the third baseman, Brandon "Lightning" Leonard, and the first baseman, Tony "Cujo" Rocca. All we are missing is the second baseman, whom none of us had met. As soon as we had run out of things to small talk about, right when the moment gets awkward, we're greeted by a tough-looking kid with, "Sup guys? You ready to kick some ass?" To which Diego replies, "Nice shirt, retard. What are you, gay? *Pff* Idiot."

"Yes, actually, I am."

He seems to notice how awkward this makes us all feel and decides to change the topic with a pleasant smile, "Well, I'm Shark and it looks like I'm going to be playing second base with you boys." None of us can tear our stares away from him as he picks up his bag, stiff wrists and all, and walks toward the boarding gate.

"There's no way he's sittin' behind me." Diego says with a sideways grin.

We then finally choose to follow him to the gate, and get on the plane. After an especially long-seeming flight spent next to Diego, I arrive in Australia. As I step off of the plane, the warm air hits me like a truck full of bricks.

"Oh, crap!" is the only phrase that comes to mind. I forgot it was summer here. My wardrobe consists of corduroy pants, fleece pullovers, and beanies.

From this exclamation, Diego, the brilliant little devil, concludes that I am an idiot, and says, "Dude, you're such an idiot."

"Thanks, Diego, I really couldn't figure that out for myself."

The coaches now decide to inform us of our room assignments. "Okay, now for room assignments: Shark, Diego, and..."

I know what the name is before he even says it.

"Mark."

So that was it, Diego, Shark, and I have to spend the next fourteen nights sleeping in the same room.

"This is going to be hell."

"You said it, bro."

I am so lost in thought that I don't even notice that everyone has left; the only people left are Shark and Diego, no doubt, waiting for the key to the room. We are all a little tired from the ridiculously long flight, and I am as eager as they are to get some rest. Only I know we won't be getting any. The night is rocked with arguments and fights whose equals I had never experienced.

For Diego, his night consists of making derogatory remarks about homosexuals, and asking if people wanted to "start a little scuffle, here."

As for Shark, his night consists of refuting the derogatory remarks and getting into those scuffles with Diego. I, on the other hand, simply get tired of getting flailing fists of fury in my face. I sleep in the bathtub after putting up with it for approximately three hours. I can only guess what went on with them.

It probably went something like this: Diego would say, "Hey, homo!"

To which Shark would reply, "Listen, man, I'm gittin' sick of this shit, back off."

This, of course, would upset Diego, because he hates to be outdone. He would surely make another remark, which I cannot repeat, and Shark would have hurt him. Now Diego would back off for a little while, until he stops crying, at least, and then go right back at it. This is the best I can do, because I'd hear yelling, fighting, and then nothing for about 15 minutes. Then it would all start again. I could have set my watch to it.

The next day, our play is horrid. Diego refuses to catch a ball thrown by Shark, for fear that he might get "cooties." This angers Shark, so he refuses to cover the base on any steals. And since I am the catcher, I start flipping out. The whole center of our field falls apart. It is as if we are playing without a catcher, short stop, or second baseman. Needless to say, but I will, nonetheless, the coaches are not very content with us three. They decide that the best course of action is to pull a "breakfast club" and lock us up in a room for six hours. I don't bring to their attention that the whole reason we had become enemies is because of the night we had just spent together, in a room, for well over six hours.

This time, however, I have a plan. I am going to use the one thing that had always given me a place, whomever I would be with, poker. Poker has the ability to take men from around the world, no matter what race or belief, and bring them together. When I first discuss the idea with Diego and Shark, they welcome my suggestion with:

"What the hell are you thinking?" says Diego.

"Diego's right, you are an idiot." adds Shark.

"Yeah, man, right on. This kid's been botherin' me since I first met him."

"You too? I thought I was the only one who didn't like him."

"No, believe me, Shark-o, nobody likes him. Hey, man, I'm really sorry about all the gay cracks and stuff. I didn't mean any of it. I say it to everybody, but now that I know somebody who is gay, I see how wrong it is. I'm really sorry."

"Don't worry about it, buddy, I'm over it."

I am getting fed up and decide to chime in with, "Hey! What about me? I didn't do anything to you guys! Our teamwork is still going to be all screwed up if you guys don't like me!"

Now, it's great that these two guys are getting along now, but what the hell? Their hatred of me brought them together. They decide that the team would not really suffer as long as I shut up and do my job. Granted, I wasn't too happy about this, I like to be liked. I shouldn't be too bitter, considering we go 8-3 the rest of the trip, and they are all close games. What really gets me is that they don't like poker. And what kind of a person doesn't like poker?

Carroll Emerson

Psalm 16 Years Old

"As I walked through the shadow of the valley of death…"
Rummaging, with thoughts of happy times,
I searched for the chord that hung from the bare light bulb.
The light was burning my heart and I felt the urge to again be in the dark.
Somehow the dark was cooling, refreshing and soothing my heart.
The light hurt it, burnt it and
made me too aware of things I did not want to know.
Things like the truth.
There was help out there somewhere, but all I wanted to see was darkness.
The darkness comforted me from the light that tried to show me the way to
where I could find the rope.
The rope was the gateway to the valley.
A valley of happiness where there was peace and quiet and trees.
A big meadow where I could do anything I wanted.
I could climb trees or buildings.
I could be alone with no one else there.
The world on this side of the valley was covering the light that hurt my eyes.
I needed to constantly close my eyes because in the light I would see nothing
that could comfort me.
I would see people shouting and yelling.
Shouting and yelling at each other.
Shouting and yelling at me.
Nobody liked me.
Nobody loved me.
Nobody cared about me.

All the light did was hurt me. There was a small cardboard box and the rope
lay on top.
Here was the key to the gate for the valley.
I took it in my hands and it was cool. I felt comforted.
I shut off the light for the first time knowing that there would be no more
light to hurt me.
I walked outside in the shadows of the cloudy day.
It was a warm early afternoon in a New England November.
I just wanted out of the light and into the valley.
My head was confused I knew what I had to do.
I no longer had to be content with the pain and the failure, I had finally
decided to make it better.
The nylon rope made it easy to make knots.
Sea cadets had taught me to tie knots, and I was good at it.
At least I was good at something.
Throwing the rope over the beam of the deck, I knew what I had to do.
I had no feelings.
I didn't feel bad.
I didn't feel sad.
I felt in control.
I fitted the rope over my neck and grabbed a stool.
The stool had always been used for sitting on.
Now it was used not for sitting but for standing.
The stool was going to be my ticket to the valley where I would feel no evil.
I kicked the stool away.
I was surprised my mind was empty.
I had always heard that people's lives flash before them, but
nothing happened.
Then the rope broke and I fell and sat all curled up in a ball.
Disappointed that I couldn't even do that right.
The sun came out and the light didn't bother me anymore.
It stole me from the valley of death…
"and surely goodness will follow me all the days of my life…"

Nancy Fang

I'm Yours

Roses are red
Violets are blue
The sky turns black
When I am reminded of you

Clouds gather overhead
As I think of what you've done
And my blood runs cold
Because you don't find fault in your actions

You think you're so clever
So smart—that I am nothing
But your god damn minion
Wrapped around your finger

That when you need something
You can smile and act nice to me
That other than that I'm useless
And you won't give me the time of day

Well, your manipulations have hit the fan
But I don't see you ducking
They will slap you in the face
And leave you keeled over in dirt

When this happens you'll turn to me
Expect me to dry your tears
And comfort your pain
But will I??

Of course
Because after all
I'm yours

Scott Fleishman

A Story For Every Day Of The Year

Tom said nothing as he let the test fall to the kitchen table. His father, Henry, glanced over the top of the *Boston Globe* as the piece of paper settled next to him. Tom stood by the door with his backpack already on. No words were needed. Tom let the three red slashes speak for themselves. The shape they formed burned through the paper, burned through the words scribbled in black ink behind it.

Henry's eyes narrowed as he lowered his coffee mug from his lips. His eyes flicked to Tom and then towards the window as he muttered a "Jesus Christ."

Tom rolled his eyes in anticipation of the argument he knew would ensue. The argument they had had so many times before. All through sophomore year, he and his father had yelled and screamed, over and over again. It always started the same way. With a tough quiz or a test after a night up with a bad cold or a couple of missed days during review. Tom would always wait for just the right moment, when there was only a few more minutes before he had to leave for school. He would sit up the night before, practicing what he would say and fantasizing about what he really wanted to say.

Henry shook his head in disgust. "Jeez Tom, school just started last week. How could you possibly have already failed a test? You've been in school for what, six days?"

Tom looked at the paper, avoiding eye contact. "Summer reading," he said feebly.

"Well did you read the damn book?"

"Dad." Tom was already feeling the frustration. "Yeah Dad, I read the book, I just, it was, like I read it, but I just didn't really get it."

"Well why didn't you ask someone for help if you didn't get it? You had all summer."

"Dad, can you just sign it?"

Henry closed his eyes and sipped from his mug. "This is a lousy start to the year. I thought it was clear how you had to act now. You're a junior, you…"

"Dad I act just fine. I don't do drugs or any of that stuff; all you care about is grades. Now I'm already late for second period. My free-block ended like a couple minutes ago and I need that signed for today. Can you just skip the talk and sign it?"

"No I can't skip the talk. It appears that last time we had this talk, you didn't really hear me. And we are going to keep having this talk until you get your damn act together."

Tom glared at his father, but had nothing to say. He could not seem to find the lines he had practiced the night before.

"We've talked about this over and over again. This is the most important year of high school. This is when you need to get the best grades and be on your best behavior if you even want to go to college."

Tom had almost recovered his lines when his brother, Steve, walked into the kitchen wrapped in a blanket. Tom turned, annoyed. "What're you doing here?"

"I'm sick," Steve said smugly.

"He's sick," Henry said as he continued to slowly sip his coffee. Steve smirked at Tom and walked into the family room. He picked up the remote and put it to MTV.

"Don't you think he's a little young to be watching rap videos? Those things are graphic."

Henry did not seem to be listening.

Steve turned his head to Tom. "I'm in middle school now, I can watch whatever I want."

"Dad, he is so not sick. Look at him."

"Tom, don't change the subject."

Steve came back into the kitchen and poured himself some cereal. "What happened? Tom flunked another test?"

"Steve, this doesn't concern you," Dad said sternly. "Stay out of it."

Tom grunted in frustration and sat down at the table. "I'm late Dad, can you just sign it?" He pushed the test closer to his dad, but Henry immediately pulled away.

"Don't you want to go to college, to have a future?"

Tom hit the table with his fist. "It's just one test."

"Yeah, now it's one test, it's only Tuesday. Who knows how many F's you'll have by Friday, let alone the end of the year."

Tom's mouth became useless as it struggled to form even one word, some kind of argument or comeback. Nothing came out.

Henry put his mug to his lips and started once again to take small, but loud sips of the dark liquid.

"God damn it Dad, would you stop with the fuckin' coffee!"

Henry froze. Steve spun around and looked at Tom in amazement. "You said," he paused, "the F-word." Steve's mouth hung open in stunned amazement.

Henry slowly lowered his mug to the table. Tom stared into the black abyss inside the mug. Anger and confusion swirled in his head like the remaining cream slowly changing shape on the surface of the coffee. No one made a sound. The dreaded word had never been uttered in the house since Tom first learned the word in third grade.

Henry turned to Steve. "Go watch TV."

Tom looked up at his dad, then retreated back to looking into the cup. "Dad, I just…"

"Never talk to me like that again," his father's voice was dead calm, but his eyes flashed with fury.

Tom did not break his gaze from the mug.

"You know not to talk like that. I am your father, you show me some damn respect."

"It's just a word. It was a…" He grunted in aggravation. "Dad, I didn't mean anything by it."

"Well, you must have meant something when you said it."

Tom impatiently gnawed at his lip. "You swear, no one yells at you."

"Tom, I'm the adult. Do not start this with me."

Tom was yelling now, "It's just a word, it doesn't matter! You always think the wrong things matter!"

Henry lifted the mug and finished off most of the coffee. He slammed it down on the table with his hand still tightly clutching the handle. "No, it is not just a word."

"I need to go to school. Second period started at 8:45. It's already ten past nine," Tom tried to suppress his frustration. "Can you please sign the test."

"Tom, we're not done here. Apologize."

Before Tom could retort, Steve ran into the kitchen with a worried look on his face. "Dad, look!"

Henry looked at Steve questioningly, then turned to the TV. Steve turned up the volume.

"Something's happened, oh my God, I can't tell but, but I think, what? Hold on, oh my God yes we have confirmed a second has struck. The screen shook as it revealed plumes of dark smoke pouring from the raging flames. Debris flew through the air and fell to the street hundreds of feet below. Dark objects seemed to move as they plummeted to the sidewalk."

Henry stiffened as he stared at the TV. His mouth was slightly ajar, and he was holding his breath. He muttered something to himself and slumped forward in his chair. His elbow slowly slid off the table. As his hand went over the side of the table, his grip loosened and the mug freed itself from his grasp. It balanced on the edge of the table then tipped. It crashed into the kitchen floor. The mug shattered, turning to fragments. The rounded handle shot across the room. Coffee splattered up Henry's leg, but he didn't seem to notice.

Henry pulled his gaze from the TV to Tom's confused face. For a moment, their eyes locked, burning into each other. The adrenaline of the argument was still pumping through Henry's veins, but he could no longer remember why they had been fighting.

"There's debris and people everywhere I can barely see oh, oh God this is horrible."

Kate Gildersleeve

Medieval Girl

In the old green tent that stood next to the fifty-foot maple tree, Maggie was curled up in her sleeping bag reading her favorite book. She was not exactly what you would call an "ordinary" teenage girl. Her light brown hair was long and wild, her thick glasses were perched on the top of her nose, and she was wearing her grandmother's wedding dress.

At her old school, Maggie was always leading a strike of some kind, or circulating a petition about the harms of dishwashing liquid. Despite her peculiarity, Maggie had friends there with whom she shared everything. Unfortunately, her friendships with these girls had been severed in half by her father's recent actions. Two days ago, she had been torn away from her small town in Minnesota and dragged to Greenwich, Connecticut. As beautiful as her new house was, Maggie was miserable. She couldn't imagine starting her life over again as it had taken her almost three years to fit into her old school. And that was in Minnesota. Maggie looked through the tent door, and up into the cloudless cerulean sky. "Perfect," she muttered. "Just like this goddamn town." Maggie shook her head, and returned to the adventurous world of Laura Ingles Wilder.

Maggie smacked the small alarm clock as it squawked impatiently at 6:45 on Monday morning. Groaning, Maggie managed to pull herself out of bed, put on her glasses, and saunter over to the gleaming mirror on the opposite corner of her room. Her hair was everywhere, her eyes refused to open, and her acne was at its peak. It was a typical day. Looking through her closet, Maggie decided on wearing her favorite dress to the first day of school. Maggie had bought it while she was at a Medieval fair with her friends. She even had a crown of flowers that matched the outfit! After slipping on the dress and the crown, Maggie headed down to breakfast.

Her mother turned around to inspect her daughter. Pamela had short brown hair, always wore a lot of make-up, and was quite pretty for her age. She always begged Maggie to put on a little lipstick, or to take more care of her appearance, but Maggie never listened.

Maggie's father lowered his glasses, banged his coffee cup down on the table, and glowered at his daughter. "Maggie, what in God's name are you wearing? We don't live in the middle of nowhere anymore! This is Greenwich! I hoped that you would at least try to fit in on your first day."

Maggie glared into his eyes just as fiercely as he had spoken. "For the hundredth time, I like this dress, and I don't care what people think of me. It doesn't matter WHERE we are, I will never try and be like everyone else."

Bob Harkins gave Maggie one more disgusted glance before turning his attention back to his coffee and the sports page of *The New York Times*.

Just as Maggie was about to sit down to breakfast, her brother walked down the stairs. Tim was the perfect child. He was friendly, intelligent, and had better manners than a prince. Of course, Pamela and Bob Harkins doted upon him endlessly. Today, like usual, he looked like he had just walked out of a photo shoot for Abercrombie and Fitch.

Maggie hated him with a passion. He was one of those typical boys whom everyone loved, no matter what they did. Pretty girls were always calling him up and coming over to the house, drooling over him incessantly. Staring at his innocent face, Maggie suddenly felt furious. She grabbed her bright orange backpack, slammed the screen door shut, and angrily set off for school.

When Maggie reached her destination, she instantly felt like she was going to be sick. The street was lined with Porches, Mercedes, and BMWs. A blond girl who was stepping out of her Z3 held her head up high and strutted past Maggie, not forgetting to push her out of her way. When Maggie struggled to regain her balance, the girl lowered her sunglasses, smirked at Maggie's apparel, and continued on her way until she reached a group of girls who looked exactly like her.

The day did not get much better. As Maggie walked down the hall, people gathered around their lockers in little clusters, pointing and laughing. In her classes, all the seats surrounding Maggie's desk were empty, as no one wanted to sit near the "weird new girl." Even her teachers looked at her under disapproving eyes.

At dinner that night, when Pamela asked how everyone's day had been, Tim immediately spoke. "It's great! I love it here! I've met so many new friends already! By the way, can I go to a party on Saturday night?"

Pamela and Bob looked at each other and smiled. "Sure, sweetie. That sounds like fun." Pamela fixed her gaze on Maggie. "And Maggie, did you have a good day at school?" Maggie's silence told Pamela the answer. "Well, Maggie, if you only would try to be more normal, well, maybe you would be having a better time."

The next day, things only got worse. Maggie's unusual attire got even more attention, and she still had not made a single friend. After eating lunch by herself, Maggie went over to her locker to put away the lunch that she hadn't finished. There, in permanent black marker were the words "GO HOME MEDIEVAL GIRL." Maggie couldn't take it anymore. She broke down in tears and bolted out of the school.

For the next two days, Maggie stayed in her tent by the maple tree. She refused to eat, drink, or communicate with anyone. On the second morning, Maggie heard her father marching out to her tent.

"Maggie, this is ridiculous. Get out of that tent NOW! You are going to school today, and I don't care WHAT you say." When Maggie stayed where she was, her father zipped open the door, grabbed her by the arm, and yanked her out. When she finally stood up, he slapped her. Hard. "That's what you get for being a stubborn little bitch."

When Maggie got to school that day, she pulled out sandpaper and a rag to clean off the vandalism on her locker. As she was kneeling on the ground scratching away the stinging phrase, she heard loud voices behind her.

"Rachel, what am I going to do with my gum? I don't see a trash can anywhere!"

"You don't, Lauren? What about that one!"

"Oh, how could I miss it? Thanks."

Maggie felt something fall on the back of her head. As she cautiously put her hand up to her precious hair, she felt something sticky that was interfering with her usual waves. Gum. As Maggie turned around in horror, she saw that Lauren and Rachel were not alone. The hallways were filled with people, who began laughing on cue. Everywhere she turned, fingers were pointed at her, as the sound of laughter filled her eardrums. A wave of panic swept over her, and Maggie started screaming. She couldn't stop. It was as if God had given her enough breath to scream forever. Shocked looks overcame the laughter as it quickly died down.

When Maggie stopped screaming, her breathing was harsh and ragged. Even though Maggie was not intending to speak, words came tumbling out of her vocal chords. "Why, why! None of you have a reason to treat me like this. I have talked to no one, said nothing to anyone. Yet I still am treated like absolute CRAP. Is it because you're threatened by me? Because I wear different clothes than what is "popular"? I don't get it. I have gone through absolute HELL in the past couple days because of you people, and you don't care at all. You don't know anything about me! Well, let me tell you something about myself. I am an individual. I am NOT a beauty queen, I do NOT go to the mall every weekend, and I do NOT care what I look like. I wear the clothes I want to wear, and act the way I want to act. I for one, am proud of who I am, which is a lot more than any of you can say about yourselves. All I ask is that you respect me for ME. Not because I deserve to be treated fairly, not because I am standing in front of all of you right now, but because I am a human being. And human beings are not supposed to be treated this way."

The halls rang with silence. A couple people coughed, but no one dared say anything. As scuffling feet moved restlessly, a teacher interrupted the scene and sent everyone to class.

At that moment, Maggie had made history. Maybe all those people who had listened to what she had to say wouldn't change their ways. Maybe they wouldn't become better people. But that day, Maggie had made them realize something. No matter how different people are, no matter how much they don't fit in, you always need to respect them for their beliefs. Maggie was never bothered again.

Michael Grodzinsky

My Shot

Last Friday
I was playing basketball
with some friends.
I was successful in
winning
against
two different people.

The leather ball seemed to
fly seamlessly
through the air,
flawlessly swishing
through the net.

I had found
my shot.

Darren Gwinn

Beating The Upperclassmen

Every Thursday morning
during X-block,
except on half days,
the underclassmen play
the upperclassmen
in basketball.

These games are very competitive.
Both sides are into the game.

But it always seems that
the underclassmen win.

It's my crossover
and my three-point shot.

Russell Hadaya

We Are All The Same

The warmth of the sun invigorates
the lively surroundings,
such as the waterfalls
forming into serene lagoons,
the endless valleys
coated with the greens of grass,
the rolling hills
teasing the wind which must
dart in and out of the slopes
created by the hills.
The animals bathe in
the warmth provided by the sun,
a platypus rolls in the sand,
fish glide through the lagoon
that the waterfalls have created.

All these events
that words cannot describe
are forbidden to those imprisoned by slavery.
Even the slaves that were born into slavery
know of freedom. The elders tell the young
about freedom and the life before slavery.
It gives them hope,
hope when there could possibly be none.

They dig down deep
to the worn thoughts
of life beyond the shackles.

The route to freedom
out of the prison of slavery
is to reveal the truth
that behind these coverings
which society puts upon us
we are all the same.

Ricky Ham

My Freedom

I think about how easy it is
to take our freedom for granted.
I think about death. I think about
all the people who lost a father,
a mother, a brother, a sister,
an aunt, an uncle, a grandfather, a grandmother,
a husband, a wife, a friend. I think about
how bad it must have been.

I treat every day with my family
as it is my last. Family and friends are
the most important things to me.

Worry is something I think about.
I feel the power of the word.
I always hear about people getting taken
from their homes or someone
getting grabbed at the park.
It happened to these people.
Why couldn't it happen to my family?

I am always worried of someone
coming and grabbing my mom while
she is shopping. I am always worried
of someone grabbing my brother while
he is out with his friends. I am always worried

of someone grabbing my dad while
he is away. I am always wondering if
someone is going to grab my two little cousins
at school or while they're out playing in their yard.
I worry about someone taking
my cousin's little sister while
she is at church or while she is in school.

I am always worried about not being there.
Always worried about not being able
to do something to help them.

Worrying is a part of my freedom.

Ben Johnson

The Runner In The Woods Meets A Friend

I was jogging through the woods. The wind was blowing in my face, and I felt cold tears running from my eyes. It was blurry in front of me, and I had to be extra careful to avoid stumbling over a rogue root or rock in my path. I suppose I was so concentrated on being alert to those obstacles that I didn't even hear the man approach.

"Where are you headed?" he asked me from behind.

I looked around, startled to hear his voice. At first, in consequence of my blurred vision, he was a haze of blue and black. But soon his defined shape came into focus, and I realized he was a nice looking man, with a cheery disposition. He was about the same height as I, wearing a blue running jacket, and black running pants. His hair was brown, and just long enough to see a hint of waviness in it.

He smiled at me as he asked again, "Where are you headed?"

"Nowhere in particular," I said, "I'll probably turn out onto the bike path in a few minutes. It's much easier to run out there than it is in here."

"Yes, that's what a lot of runners do when they run through here." He said this with the air of an expert on the topic of runners. "They like how the bike path is straight, and paved, and there aren't so many stumbling obstacles along the way."

I agreed with him, and told him about how I didn't even hear him coming because of how alert I was being to those stumbling obstacles.

"Yea, you've got to be careful out here. But then again, you've got to be careful on the bike path too. You know, once I was running on the bike path, and I tried passing this one runner, but you know what he did? As soon as I got beside him, and he saw I was trying to pass him, he told me I shouldn't. And when I didn't back away, he shoved me into the trees along the bike path."

I acknowledged that I had almost had an accident on the bike path too, and then went on to tell him about how once I had been running on the bike path, and I almost tripped over a dead squirrel that was lying in the middle of the path.

"You see! That's the kind of stuff I'm talking about here! You can't trust these woods for safe running; you can't trust the bike path for safe running! So where can you find some safe running?"

"I don't know." I said, feeling kind of dumb with such a simple answer.

"I'll tell you where." He said. "Follow me; it's a little up the way. There's this beautiful long path, through a field that has never been touched, except by me. It's straight as an arrow, not a rock or root in site, just smooth sailing. Or smooth running I should say. I guess we aren't sailors are we?"

I smiled at this comment. The man was very pleasant and inviting. I decided that I might as well follow him. If the path turned out to be less than what he said, I could simply turn around and go back to the bike path.

So, on we ran.

It wasn't very far until we took a left turn down a path, which until that day, I had never noticed before. Not long after the turn, the trees became less dense, and soon we were fully immersed in a yellow and green field. The two of us ran side by side down the center of the field, on the path that the man had described. Tall waving grass was on either side of us, about waist high. The sun was shining very brightly, and not a cloud was in the sky. There was no need to look at the ground for roots or stones, because not even a fluctuation in the dirt was visible. Soon this field had some strange and intoxicating effect on me, and I suddenly felt free and joyous! I speeded up, and passed my companion in a rush of wonderful adrenaline. I felt as though I was no longer running, but flying, and infinity was my limit. But then my spirits plummeted as I suddenly felt the ground beneath me disappear, and I looked down to witness my feet stepping uncontrollably into a murky hole about twice my height. I fell face first but did a half flip and landed on my back. The fall wasn't as painful as it could have been, but it hurt a lot even so. I did not dare get up, with the fear of hearing a snap in my back or arm. I decided to wait for the man, hoping he'd be along soon to help.

Within about two minutes my spirits were lifted as my friend peaked his head over the top of the hole. "Are you okay?" he shouted.

"I think so, but I'm not going to move, just in case. Go get some help!"

"I'll be back as soon as possible."

And with that his head was gone.

An hour went by, and he didn't return. I kept as calm as I possibly could, down in that hole. Another hour went by, and then another, and another. I passed the time by watching the clouds, far up above.

By what must have been my fifth hour in the hole I decided to get up, and sure enough, I heard a painful snap, and I lied back down. Now I was dirty, in pain, and lying in a hole. I was starting to doubt that man would ever be back to rescue me. I would be stuck in this hole forever.

Despair started to cloud my mind, but horror soon replaced it when I realized that I had been feeling raindrops for the past several minutes. Then the horror was solidified as it started pouring the rain down in trenches. The dirt started turning to slippery mud, and sliding down all around me. It soon covered my chest and was creeping up to my face. Within moments I felt the terrible taste of mud in my mouth, and soon I could feel it in my nose and in my ears. And then the rain came down and down, never even considering the man it was now drowning. Oh what a different story my life would have been, if only I had taken the bike path.

Why did I trust my friend?

Julie Kim

Divorce

A girl named Jackie had a nice family. She lived in Billerica, Massachusetts. She was nine years old. She was a wonderful person. One time when she was sitting in bed in the hospital, her parents argued. One person was on each side of her. This was not the only time that her parents fought. They fought more after she got out of the hospital. After that time when they were fighting, her parents were never at the hospital at the same time.

Jackie's parents were fighting because her father was having an affair. He had been seeing her before the fights, and her mother had found out because he came late from work every single day. Since he did not have work on Sundays, he would go out for three hours or so. Her parents were screaming at each other when they were fighting.

After a year of her parents' fighting, they got divorced during the summer of 1994. Jackie was away on vacation with her sister and her father. They went somewhere out of the nation. Jackie's father went because he wanted her mother to sign the sheet for divorce, since her mother was where they were going on vacation.

Jackie's life changed because she was living with only one parent and not able to see her other parent. She was living with her father because she only wanted one child and not the other, but Jackie's father only wanted her to take all the children or none at all. Jackie had two sisters. Jackie felt so sad; she was also depressed. She missed her mother ever since she left. Jackie cried really hard when her mother left. Her older sister cried too. Her older sister had to do all the food shopping and had to bring her younger sister to dance every week. Jackie's younger sister did not remember many things about the divorce because her sister was too young. Her grandmother helped with most of the housework.

Jackie was in the hospital because she had gotten a brain tumor and had surgery on her head. She was not able to see well because the tumor was right behind her eye. Jackie was starting to get better when her parents began fighting. Sometimes Jackie thinks that the sight of one eye was lost when one parent was lost in the heart. But she knows that it was not her fault that they got divorced. She had always cried when she thought about this story. But she never told it to anyone. This event was too sad and depressing for her to tell anyone.

Lisa Klane

Who Are You And Who You Are

I hate you.
My hate is strong, but somehow you are stronger.
You dribble, slowly into people's minds.
Carefully invading and infecting.
You affect my life with ultimate strength,
Luckily less than the actual me.

You had set in early in her mind,
plaguing her for years,
You crept in and took over.
Took over all of her thoughts, the present,
those friends, the past,
her actions, the future.
You took her away,
away from me and with you for some time.
But, she broke free from you, and came back to me.

You had been busy all along wrenching someone else.
You won him over, like a disease on a host.
You should have been satisfied with that pain
but no, you transcend the generations.
I know that you are in his head.
Peeking in and out of his thoughts, the present,
and those people, the past,
But not his actions, not his future.
He will not go with you,

I will not let him.
Get Out!

You bastard.
That is who you are,
no one could want you as their child,
you thing, you vicious, unforgiving, writhing thing,
No one wants you.

                      Sometimes I do, sometimes I want you.
                          I want you to come and me to go
                              with you, away, forever.

but You and I misjudged me,
I am strong
I will be stronger than you
and we can beat you.
Do not try to hide behind things like
stress, family, anxiety, school or even depression.

I know who you are
and I know you well

Suicide.

Stansilav Kostarnov

The Wonders Of The Night Mind

1.

The wind blew wildly in the rocks, the clouds raced by. It seemed like the rocks would be destroyed by the waves that, like giants tired of a day's work, rolled heavily onto the deserted beach. Spray flew solemnly into the night air.

Then the sight fades again. What is this? Where? The feelings of joy and sadness were all mixed up.

I started to wonder, thoughts were like waves flowing unrelated to time into the ever-deepening abyss of yearning. They rolled over me in cool, refreshing strokes. They gave me peace of mind but also invigorated me.

Light starts to fade outside or, though it's strange, outside of what? Does it fade for we are in no capsule and live in our own within the light? The next thought comes. Which of these worlds is real? Certainly the one on the other side of the barrier...or maybe?

2.

Why can't we reason when we are in the world that's solid? Maybe it's our senses that don't let our minds float freely when awake. Our minds cannot, in here, react and relate to the solid reality. But why in reality can it relate to this world of liquid and thought that is as fog revealed to a clear mind.

Nature is wise for it will provide you with time to think over all you need. Yet too often we do not think enough of the things of most pure importance in our lives. Only bread for the spirit gives life its satisfaction and will quench the burning hungers for truth.

Yes, and memory too is for me best served not of those places that have the best food, hotels or scenery, but of those where friends seemed closest. These places were target camp, Crimea and others that, in this manner, brought relief to the mind. The friends were of totally different types, but all very close to my heart.

3.

As I lay there on the cold rough gloomy stones, I hear a voice calling me with him. I get up and start walking. This man I know well, though I met or saw him not before. As we walked through the ages among the great boulders of time and life, we entered a second being from which few details can I recall. My mind was covered with thought, as if what it was could never be recovered. But as thought came through though and covered itself in a knot, the time, like a wet string, slipped out of my hand, with it untying the silk of memory spun by the spiders of our senses.

As the moments flash by, the dream must end. But it does not, for the unfamiliar world must persist.

The unknown yet so familiar man walks in front of me and then, like a weary apparition, a huge lake appears before us. The old man slowly walks towards it, as if fearing the disappearance of the new wonder into the water-saturated air that, in the form of mist, tricks our senses. Then, out of the fog, appear oaks, their silhouettes coming from the darkness of distance. These oaks were as old as the age itself, as tall as the towers of Italy and as wise as the greatest of men and as terrible as any of the wolves of the North.

The oaks stood draped in the brown shrouded cloaks of last year's leaves, solemn and sad in the rain. Yet from them went an unmistakable joy of being among the Great Century thinkers.

The trees were not heading for the sky. Their arms were few and heavy. Their trunks were as twisted as the snaking ways of the mind. Yet there was power in these hard trouble-worn muscleless bodies, for their branches were frozen in a swing and the trunk was yet ready to pounce. They were in an infinite sleep that brought wisdom of an equal amount.

This sleep, however, did not come monolith out of the deep of night, but trickled in from the soul of the tree and covered its branches with a blue fog of hope. There was a quiet crunching sound and, as in a slow-motion film, the branch of the oldest of all the trees fell to the ground, producing a thump that split the air and was repeated by a chorus of a million echoes.

The trees were not alive, but were still bursting with personality, only pockets of life were left upon their mighty branches. The birth out of the dead wood of the green leaves was a process that's pleasant to watch. It was brought into Nature to bring about hope, and it does that successfully, for that duty is its most favored task.

Those trees indeed were great and indeed they had been thinking all their time. As we stood there, the trees shook off the rain of the morning and started bathing in the afternoon sun.

We walked up to the lake. The water was mirror-like. It seemed not a grain of sand was misplaced in the whole lake. It seemed as if it were some symbol of peace.

Then darkness falls again, a small light appears, fog swirls around some peak, a dark abyss opens below my feet, figures move around on a small road far down. Somehow I knew there was a valley and a river below, but all that was now infinitely far. Only a knowledge remained that anything else existed.

I saw people determined in their challenge to make the dark a little lighter. They were tugging ropes, ropes of hope, ropes of work. They were tearing the rocks of the Great Body of the Mountain, plucking out its dark and eroded heart.

Thoughts followed the same pattern as the scenery. They were not serene, they weren't flowing over in wavelike cool gusts. The thoughts hammered down in a wild torrent, as if they echoed the ever-running avalanche of darkness that now engulfed us both. We fell through the darkness like a stone, lost to the world above, yet found by the richness of that which was below.

Around me was a swirling moist current of gloom. Though the rocks below were sharp as razors, no fear was in sight. Then the scenery changed. A light-blue fog covered all, a river trickled. We were sitting in a circle. Me, a tall looking man in a jacket, a strange-looking bearded man of about forty in a black anarack, and the old man in his normal torn black tunic. A broth was cooking in the old pot on a fire in a hole in the ground. The darkness was ultimate, as if the eyes had no knowledge of what was outside the small wooden gazebo.

Again "the game" started, a distant noise of unicorn feet was driving the peaceful world into a circle around my body. The echo of past waves appeared to have come back and the abyss flashed by. There was no bridge to the island which appeared. A black shape glided through the darkness. Its wings seemed to cut the rich and cold night air. Out of the night came a new image, a new idea maybe, it was flying in a circle around me like a bat and yet I could not grab it, though its route seemed identical to that of my hand.

In the distance, thunder rolled as clear as if somebody beat a drum a few meters away, and yet none could see darkening clouds. The countryside around seemed to live a life separate from the reality. From a thousand caves infinitely above us, there was a howl of creatures unknown to man and unseen to other inhabitants of the earth.

They danced the dark sky and the oaks that we mentioned in this story before were among them, their minds enlightening the world with a trillion stars of knowledge. This was indeed the time when the dream, after it has tested your reaction to it, comes in its full power to take every resource of imagination and show you its theme.

It comes in a slow but steady gallop in its many billions of images, and yet it may just be like the moon that watches it from behind the cloudy veil, not fully ever revealing itself, and then disappears leaving no image of itself in the brain or the heart. Its Great Flame, however, dwindled in the sky, and under its warmth the countryside was ever mobile in the face of the setting moon. The world of that outside human knowledge was ever more present, its cat-like eyes staring at our gazebo that stood in the flow of the clean river water which invisibly linked the far off mountains to the dark stormy sea. All was now quiet, so quiet that you could hear a pin fall onto the unending plateau of leaves and needles. This was the final episode of the adventure; the boats were ready and the dream's challenge had been met and the time for the end had come. I had already gotten to know this world very well. In fact, though somewhere I knew I must be awakening, I could not recall a world outside of it.

The boats were untied and the old man with the torn coat bid me goodbye. I looked with light sadness at an unrealistic world that would soon cease to exist. The boats had already disappeared into the morning fog and the vision that I so loved disappeared too. A new world would be made the next night, but for now my time was up and a rising sun shone through the window.

4.

Few will enter that world of the wild free mind, because it's the mind, not the sense, that may discover it. The measurement of the mind is not sensible for mathematical calculations, and is therefore greater by far. Its unlimited freedom mocks the powers of sanity for they, in all their logic, overlap, contradicting each other. Nothing that cannot be convinced through faith is true for a man who sees infinity will uncalculate his own existence as not true. Only by our beliefs do solids take on a physical sense, whilst dampness, like darkness, is felt through the heart.

We don't know we are we. We say it's unlimitedly likely, but our senses never allow us to doubt our existence, though we can't prove it to any alienated mind. We, by our evil instincts, will be perceived as the mad men, while their theory is much more logical than that of existence. In our "true" world we perceive in unison, imprisoning the brain in a cage of reality, and only Dali will lift our world on his mind's crutches, through the mist of suspicion.

Zach Lager

The Pitch

The smell of freshly cut grass,
The birds chirping,
The fans in lawn chairs,
The dirt blowing in the warm breeze,
The sweat glowing on players' faces,
The taste of sunflower seeds,
The hotdogs,
The spitting,
The ballpark,
The dugout,
The players,
The gloves,
The bats,
The teams,
The beautiful round sphere with red stitched seams,
THE PITCH

Though the game doesn't start for another two hours, I start my preparation way ahead of time. I think about how I will approach different situations, how I will pitch to certain players, how I hope to be successful, and what I will have to do to be able to accomplish all of this. I slowly start to put on my uniform thinking about my mechanics and those things my coach has often told me I had to do: "Keep your head level, whip your torque and bring your glove hand into your body for more power, don't overthrow, and alternate the location of your pitches." Dressed and ready, I head to the game.

I arrive about a half hour early and walk around the field, feeling the warm spring breeze, the sun shining on my back, the smell of the freshly cut grass, and the diamond of dirt with the mound in the center of it all. Walking to the pitching mound, I envision myself pitching in the game, throwing strikes, getting outs—winning the game. I walk over to the bench, sit down and lace up my cleats. Other players slowly arrive, and talk of the game buzzes through the air. The team jogs around the field, and we then situate ourselves in the outfield where we stretch and warm-up. About this time, the opposing team arrives, and there's the reason we all play the game, TO WIN!

The team goes through its pre-game warm-ups. Everyone can hear the chatter from the players:

"Nice play kid."

"What da'ya say John"

"Nice catch!"

The whole team is focused on the game ahead; everyone knows his job and what he has to do. Each player knows that the minute you zone out, the minute you lose track of the number of outs, the minute you don't know who is on base and where, that is the minute that the ball is hit to you and you make a mistake, costing your team and your cause. While my teammates are taking their warm-ups in the field, I am in the bullpen warming up for the game. I mix in curve balls, fastballs, and change-ups on both the inside and outside corners, all the while preparing both physically and mentally for the game. I believe that most of pitching is concentration, competitiveness, and confidence. With these three factors the mental part of pitching is taken care of. The pitcher always has to believe he can "do it"; the pitcher always has to concentrate solely on the present and never on the past; and the pitcher always has to compete to be the best, to strike out the best, to outsmart the best.

It is finally time! The game is about to begin. I have my pre-game jitters, as I always do, but I know that the second I set foot on the mound these nerves will all melt away and nothing will matter except me, the batter, and the ball. Our team huddles, yells "Win!" and the starting lineup runs out to their positions.

"Play Ball!" the ump signals me, telling me it is time. I walk up to the mound, dig my feet into the soft, gushy dirt, and peer at my catcher's signals. He holds up one finger, telling me to throw a fastball. I nod my head, telling him that I agree. I place the ball in my hand, moving it around until I can feel that perfect grip. Those bumpy red seams feel like extensions of my fingers. I come to my set with ball in hand and hand in glove, while focusing on the catcher's glove. Throughout my motion, I never look at my opponent, only at the glove. This keeps me focused and does not allow me to be intimidated by the batter. I cock my arm back, kick my leg up, push off, and release the ball—the pitch. It streams toward the inside corner of the plate. "STRIKE."

This is what pitching is all about—that one second when you beat your opponent, that one second that you know you have outsmarted your opponent, that one second that you know you have just thrown the perfect pitch!

Jullyce Martinez

Nathalie

I know how it feels to lose your child
It's a very bad feeling
It's a very big knot inside your chest
that you wouldn't even believe it.

On July 1st 1995,
I was the happiest aunt alive.
My sister gave birth to the niece I call my daughter
Her name is Nathalie and I am all for her.

She weighed 7 lbs. 6 oz.
with black silky hair.
I picked her up and she smiled at me
and I told her that I would always be there.

She's growing up now, a second grader in school;
she's smart enough
and gets good grades
but sometimes acts a fool.

I used to see her every day
but now she lives with her mom
When I go home she's not there
I feel kind of glum.

The love I have for her will never end
she's always with me in my heart
although sometimes she's far away.
I know we'll never be apart.

She will always be my "daughter"
she will always be my niece.
I love my baby so much
that at times she leaves me without speech.

I know she will soon grow up
and be a woman of her own.
my baby's growing up too quick
and now she thinks she's grown.

I love you boobie...from your second mom (titi).

Daniela Martinelli

September 11th

1.

As the fog sets in on the town that's covered in darkness, the clouds block out the sun which would brighten up everything it touches. On September 11th it was like the fog had settled on the United States. On that day at 8:40 A.M., New York's smiling faces that were like that brightening sun turned into frowns which were the clouds and fog.

When I had first heard of this, I was in school in the Resource Room. People were walking around crying and were very sad. Then, as I found out what had happened, I also became sad because my friend worked right across from the World Trade Center. As soon as I came home, I talked to him and found out that he wasn't near it.

September 12th, it was very hard for people to do what they used to do before September 11th. Days turned into weeks, weeks turned into months in which people were scared. People wouldn't fly because of what happened; the stock market dropped; people didn't do anything. I was scared to do my regular activities. You always had to watch what you were doing because there were threats on T.V. which scared people so much that they stayed inside. I had felt that everyone's sadness was bringing me down and that I had been scared too long, so I went out and did what I used to. I couldn't take everyone's sadness much longer. I felt that I had to make people happy.

This summer I am going to Italy, and I am a little scared to fly not knowing what's going to happen. As it gets closer and closer, I am getting nervous. But I can't let that stop me from going and having fun with my family. What has happened we cannot change or let it stop us from doing what we used to. We need to push away the fog and darkness and let the sun come out to brighten up everyone.

2.

I found out my sister was having a baby.
I had received a phone call during the day.
I was at home watching TV.

My sister told me that
I was having another nephew
which was going to be
my godchild.

3.

Last summer I was excited to tutor
at Bowman School. I love children.
And the chance to teach them? I just took it.

When I got there I was nervous.
But once I got used to them
and they got used to me
I wanted to stay there.

Laura Mauriello

In The End

Drawing the same shapes, unsatisfying
I've memorized what to do, not even thinking
I crumple the paper, tears drip down my face
My pencil darkens your eyes, your lips
Smoothing the edges
Sun floods the window, your face feels warm
Different
I crumple the paper again, it's hard to decide

Over and over again, the soft curves
All I know is your face, even when you've disappeared
Memorizing every inch, my pencil captures
Every detail, I promise not to forget
I'll take in everything, you're all I think about
Inspiring the moves of my hand, you'll see
Only when I finish

It's nothing new, I wish it could be
Just the same, the ordinary
Why can't it be real
Why won't your eyes look the way I want them to
I hate the way you stare at me
You're not helping at all
The paper's crumpled once again
It'll never be the way I want it to
In the end

Corey Merrill

A Cup Of Joe

Some nights I just like to go out and drive by myself with the music turned up loud. A few weeks ago I had one of those nights. I'd had a horrible day at school, a fight with my best friend, parent problems, and a lot on my mind. So, after dinner I grabbed the keys to my '93 Honda Accord and took off.

I was soon heading south on Route 128. The stars were out, and I turned up "Sweet Home Alabama" on the radio and reached for the half-eaten Snickers bar on the dashboard. Things were looking better—I had music, chocolate, and the open road all to myself. But about twenty minutes later I looked down at the fuel gauge and realized that I was almost out of gas. I guess that figures; usually when I'm the most worn down my car is running on empty too. After a sigh of annoyance I drove until I saw a sign for a gas station and diner and took the exit. After filling up my car with gas, I decided I might as well get something to eat, so I walked over to Chuck's Diner. I pushed open the door and walked past a gumball machine and an ashtray, through a small foyer and over a dirty "Welcome" mat. There were red vinyl booths on both sides of me, and a long white counter straight ahead with red vinyl stools to sit on. A few people sat scattered in different booths, but the counter was empty, so I went over to it and sat down. The place was lit by harsh, florescent lights, and the smell of deep fried food made my stomach turn. I was flipping through the songs on the mini jukebox at the counter when a heavy-set, middle-aged man wearing a greasy apron stretched over his potbelly appeared from behind the counter. When he handed me a wrinkled grease-stained menu, and I wondered why the place wasn't called "Grease Pit" instead of "Chuck's Diner," but I figured it would be too rude to ask.

"That's all right, I don't need a menu. I'll just have coffee," I told him. He seemed to fit right in with the diner. His greasy brown hair was thinning, and he was growing it longer to compensate. Aside from the apron he wore, he had on brown pants that were held up by a black belt, and a white button down short-sleeved shirt that was tucked into his pants. His shirt was thin and cheap and I could see the wife-beater that he was wearing under it. He seemed a little sweaty, and I was glad I hadn't ordered any food. "It's always good to know exactly what you want," he responded, and proceeded to introduce himself.

"My name's Joe," he told me as he handed me a mug of steaming coffee. "You seem like you need someone to talk to so I figured I'd introduce myself."

"Oh," I replied, not quite sure what to say. "I'm Alise."

"Alise, huh? That's a pretty unusual name, but it's nice." After an awkward silence when he just stood behind the counter and I was just hoping he'd go away and leave me to myself, he asked, "So what brings you here at night all alone?"

I was kind of irritated by his chatter when I only wanted to sit and sulk about my bad day, but I replied, "Oh, um, I just wanted to get out of the house. You know, parents and stuff, they can really get on your nerves." Hoping that he would take the hint that I didn't want to have a conversation, I stared down at my coffee and stirred it a little.

"Yeah, I understand the parent trouble," he told me. "My parents used to nag me all the time. It can really get to you after a while." I unwillingly continued to have small talk with him and ended up telling him that I was seventeen, sick of high school, and only wanted to make it to summer vacation. He told me he understood, but that he wished he could be seventeen again so he could redo everything he did wrong.

"What do you mean by that?" I asked him to be polite.

"Well," he said, "I have one big regret. I didn't finish high school, so I couldn't go to college. I dropped out when I was seventeen, and my parents made me leave the house because of it. So I've been working odd jobs ever since. I'm 38 now—Hell, I've been working at Chuck's for three years."

"So why'd you do it?" I asked.

"Well, I was so young that I had no idea what I was really doing," he told me. He left it at that, unwilling to continue.

"Oh, I understand," was all I replied.

"Did you have a bad day or something?" he asked me after a short silence.

"That's the understatement of the year," I answered. "I had the most horrible day ever." I proceeded to tell him about the huge fight my best friend Lauren and I had gotten into at lunch today, about how when I told her she couldn't copy my homework, she blew up at me. Then I told him about how my parents are always on my case about my grades and how they think I don't study enough, when they just don't understand how hard school is today.

"Parents don't understand anything, I swear. They're only around to make your life more complicated and miserable." In a downward spiral of self-pity I added, "My life sucks."

After a long pause Joe said to me, "You know, you have it really good. It's just too bad you don't know it."

"What's that supposed to mean?" I snapped at him.

"Well, at least you have a family. I come from a broken home. At least you have friends to fight with; some kids don't. You're still in school, and you even have your own car. You are so lucky. There are always going to be problems with everything—be grateful that your problems aren't so serious. Try to look on the bright side; look at what you do have." I couldn't believe I was hearing all this from a man I didn't even know. He was making me feel worse with his guilt-trip about how my problems were so trivial.

"Yeah, okay," was all I said as I paid the check and stormed out of the diner. I slammed the car door shut, and muttered, "What a jerk" before starting the engine. What did he know about my life anyway? Who did he think he was telling me all that? My life was a lot harder than he thought it was.

In an attempt to take my mind off my conversation with Joe, I turned on the radio. I was flipping though the stations trying to find something worth listening to when I heard the name "Courtney Miller" on a news station. Courtney Miller? She went to my high school, so why was she on the news? The report continued: "Courtney Miller who attended Katonah High School was returning home from Lewisborough when her car skidded on a gravel road, spun out of control, and hit a telephone pole. It appears that she died immediately after the impact. She was found at four o'clock this afternoon. There was no one else in the car with her. Details of a memorial service will be announced later in Katonah."

I couldn't believe it. I never really got to know Courtney, but she was in my grade at school, and I knew who she was. Her father had died a few years ago, and she lived with her mother and sister, who she didn't get along with. She didn't have many friends, and people considered her a loner. Although she was pretty smart, her family would have trouble paying for college, so her options were limited. When you live in a town as small as Katonah, you know a lot about everyone.

Now she was gone. Killed in a stupid accident. Why hadn't I taken the time to make friends with her? Why had I ignored her in the halls, never saying hi? I turned the radio off and drove the rest of the way home in silence. It was hard to think clearly, but I remembered what Joe had told me earlier that night. "You are so lucky…be grateful your problems aren't so serious. Try to look on the bright side, look at what you do have." I realized suddenly that Joe was right. I am lucky. I have friends and family and a bright future to look forward to, unlike a lot of people. Courtney didn't have that, and now she never will. Joe didn't have it easy either. How had I been so blind to everything I had? It had taken a conversation with a high school dropout, and a tragic event to make me realize my own good fortune. I decided to take Joe's advice and be thankful for what I have, and to try to think more about others, rather than just my own problems. When I finally made it home, tears of sadness for Courtney and shame for myself blurred my vision. I went to my room but couldn't fall asleep. I had too much to think about.

It's amazing how your life can change so much in just one day.

Julia Metzger-Traber

Marionette Footprints

Oh the sound of music
not like Julie Andrews
live
vivid
loud
the sound you can see
the emotion you can hear
the notes pull the salted water capsules down your flushed cheeks
your heart loves the object of the musician's affection
why don't you return his love?
you ask
why can't I be loved like that?
you wonder
the notes speak for themselves
they tap dance on your heart strings like the musician's very own
marionettes
he plays a chord and closes his eyes
you remember last summer
one distinct moment in time envelops you in its reality
it is real
the sun beats on your back
the grass tickles your legs
the laughter skips in your ears
and then you hear it
the guitar next to you
I miss last summer

the moment spits you back out
but leaves footprints on your soul
the flats and sharps fly around the room
sending
innocent
unsuspecting audience members
into moments of their own
the pain hurts again
the love bubbles
the music lives
he gives it a pulse
you give it a meaning

Ryan Moore

Miracle In The Sky

Toasty warm in my mummy bag

Frigid air rushing across my face
Voices awaken me to get up and stare into space

Crouching under canvas dome
The zipper feeling as cold as chrome

Piercing wind makes me shake
I don't long to be awake

Glowing embers beckon me
They provide warmth and light to see

Awestruck while looking up
Shooting stars in the giant black cup

Stars streaking across the sky
Each comet beginning to die

Flashes of light moving in every direction
Truly a miracle deserving reflection

Ball of gas speeding as a shooting star
Seemingly so close, but yet so far

The shower is growing old
As I become increasingly cold

Quickly returning to my tent
I feel my time was well spent

Charlotte Morse-Fortier

Missing My Sandbox Days

Growing up can be such a disappointing and wistful process. Our childhood is gently pulled from us like a security blanket, leaving us chilled. The pre-school years, where everyone has the same number of crackers for snack, are over too soon.

Once everyone played on the same sunny playground, used the same crayons, formed shapes from the same salty play dough. We never had to decide things for ourselves then, for we were wrapped in our comforting sameness. Now we are all going off in different directions, searching for things that we like and are good at and could get us into Columbia. Where we used to seek common ground, games we could play together, now we seek to distinguish ourselves, to be individuals. There seems to be nothing but choices, each one taking us farther away from the cozy childhood years and towards a coolly rational adulthood. As we struggle to succeed in the large world of grownups, we forget our snug security blanket years and the ease with which we greeted life.

What happened to the power we once had over our smooth warm worlds? Suddenly they expand outside ourselves to a vast expanse of humankind where we feel we can never make an imprint. When we realize that we share the planet with billions of other people, it can be hard to feel important. Does it have to be this way? Does growing up have to be so anti-climactic? Maybe we just need to pull out our picture books and footsie pajamas and really remember what it was like. Instead of mourning what we had, maybe we can find a way to bring the light and warmth of our childhood into our new life.

Shayne Osborne

Just Write

You can
take anything
around you

and turn it into
personal writing—

just how you feel
about things,

about things you
want to do

that may be
hard to do

but you want to do them
anyway,

no matter how the odds
are stacked against you.

Just write.

Just let yourself
see what you

want to write about
let it stir in your mind
flow through
your body
in your arm
through your
hand into
your
pencil
and
on
to
your
paper.

Sarah Parrish

My Little Sister

I wish that there could have been a way
For me to not have let you down
That I owned the only heart that broke
When I went crashing to the ground.
I wish that you had not invested
All your little faiths in me
That there was someone else around
That was the one you wanted to be.
I wish you hadn't bought my shoes
Laced your skates up just like me
Painted yourself a different color
So you wouldn't have the blue to see.

You didn't know that I was still growing
Young and naive, just like you
That I was just as easily broken
That my dreams could be shattered too.
So in your awkward shoes you sit
And you do not know what to do
If the big girl couldn't do it
Now you wonder, how can you?

So I am sorry I let you down
I'm sorry if your hopes are crossed
And I hope that following in my footsteps
Hasn't made you
very lost.

James Pulley

November Dad

The earliest memory I had of him was June in Raleigh,
North Carolina. We went to visit his mom.
He was adopted and he always told me he felt close to her.
He took me fishing, driving for a little bit and we caught supper.
He was about 6 foot one and had dimples that he gave to me.
It was October and Mattapan was our first house and
we lived upstairs from my aunt.
I remember the Halloween party and we bobbed for apples
and he didn't bob 'cause it was a kid thing.
Him and mom organized.
He laughed, took pictures and enjoyed himself—
and so did I.
He worked in a paper factory and left every day and
in August would bring home ice cream from
Seymours next door to his work.
He liked orange sherbet and I liked chocolate.
I still like chocolate and he probably still likes sherbet
but I don't really know.
We moved in May and for 7 or 8 years lived in Dorchester. It
was better and we were happier there, that is
the kids. Me, Jamal, and Shauna were happier.
Mom and Dad seemed to be fighting a lot. I was at my cousins' house and
I would come home in
the middle of a July afternoon and they would be fighting.
He always said no matter what we fight about it's not about you kids.
Mom and Dad didn't

organize anymore. He didn't take pictures. He didn't enjoy himself.
He would spend a couple of
days at Bernie's house in September, we wouldn't see him, and
then he would come and talk. We
would be happy to see him and I thought he'd be staying but
the fighting would start again.
Now the ice cream was from the supermarket and my mom would get it not
him.
This time he went to Bernie's and didn't come back. That was
in December.
We started to get our stuff
together in January as my mom got really aggravated and
we ended up moving in February. In
March we were at the new house and I had to say goodbye to the "FAB" gang.
The kids that kept me happy. April brings Jamal's birthday and there was no
dad.
Two more seasons passed and still no dad.
In November he called, had a new place and we visited him and we had a
good time.
Later in November I even went to work with him.
It's now spring and six months later, alone, I still remember my November dad.

Marcus Richardson-Smith

I Had Fun

Beating the
Upperclassmen

In basketball
On Thursday,

How we
Killed them

The first game,
Having 50 people

Just watching us
Pass, dribble and

Shoot, made us feel
Very comfortable,

Knowing
We were going to

Sweep them
2–0.

Robert

Shadowed By My Father

The blue light from the police vehicle bounces across the cedar deck of the colonial house with beige clapboards and a peach colored front door. Darkness came quickly to 483 Mill Ave. both inside and outside the house. Police lights were the only light in such a dark tale the teenager relayed to the detective. Detective Douglas asked the 15 year old high school student to go for a walk away from the chaos of the crime scene.

"So what happened that started all this?" inquired the tall wide shouldered detective.

Fearful and unable to answer, he barely hears the question and continues walking. Again he realizes the officer is talking to him.

"Hey, son did you hear what I said?" again probing for some connection that will help the investigation.

"I was in my bedroom with Hiccup. We always slept together. Mom and Dad gave it to me on my fifth birthday because I had trouble sleeping. My monkey and I had just gone to bed when Hiccup heard a slam. We heard it before, but didn't know what it was. Afraid to leave our bed, we decided to listen and not move. The sound got louder and our hearts were racing. A shriek caused Hiccup to leap from the bed pulling me along. We looked out the door and darted to Mummy's room for safety. I pushed open the door, and Mummy was on the ground making crying sounds, and daddy was pushing a pillow on her face. He goes to grab Hiccup, and we both run to my room."

Detective Douglas removes his coat and places it on the boy's shoulders as he shivers and slows his walk. Stopping almost as quickly as he started, the boy is silent. They turn and walk back toward the cruiser and the flashing light reflects in the glasses of the detective, and the young adolescent quickly responds:

"I was at Kurt's house and his parents dropped me off. I had called for a ride, but the answering machine came on, so I figured they were asleep. I went to grab some ice cream in the kitchen, but before I even entered the kitchen, I heard that unbearable slam and started shaking. Dashing to the stairs, I took them two at a time. The slam became louder and louder. I reached the bedroom door breathing heavily. Wanting to open the door, something held me back. A muffled scream scared me into charging through to see my mother again on the floor, shadowed by my father. Stricken with fear, I didn't know what to do. In a glance, my father rushed over to me and grabbed my arm. I whacked my father behind his head as hard as I could with my fist, and he fell to the floor. In a second everything went silent. My mother was on the floor, injured at the hands of my father. My father was unconscious."

Stephanie Smith

When You Love Someone

When you love someone so much you will do anything for them.

You will cry the cry, you will laugh the laughs, you will fight the fights,
but you will never forget the endless nights.

The love we share is very rare.
The care is there and there is nothing ever to fear.

On May 23 we opened a door.
We joined as one and the fun had just begun.

The summer was hard for we were both apart, but by fall it was all a new start.

Friday nights he would come over and we would cuddle and talk
as we mentally prepared for his big assault.

30 is his number,
I would watch him from afar,
as he would tackle and hit his men hard.

The fall came and went, but number 30 stayed near, for winter would soon
be here.

December 16th we both shall never forget, for we opened a second door that
we both will
always remember.

The love for each other grows stronger, as the next couple of weeks grow longer.

He is black and I am white, people find this to be a great sight.
They talk and they stare but trust me there is nothing to fear.

For I am in love, this I have no question of. We are together and it may not be forever but
for now we are and we care and share everything with each other.

When you love someone so much you will do anything for them.

Ian Stewart

A Round Of Golf

I drop my hand to the ground. It sweeps across the damp grass, the thin roots. The quick breeze blowing at my face dries the sweat off my forehead. It's picking up now. The surrounding trees start to bend as I line up the putt. The late sun is setting and only now do I feel its warmth on my skin. Twenty yards away lies the small hole. The line looks pretty straight. The ball is slightly shining. I pick the ball up and wipe off specs of grass. Slowly, I place the ball down, lining its emblem toward the hole. I'm crouching behind the ball as low as I can, my knees aching. I double check the ball's path, this time back from the hole toward the ball.

I wake up early this summer morning. Most of my friends are gone on vacation, and the rest, well they're working. The forecast calls for some showers, and late afternoon sun. The perfect golf day? I'd say so. On warm, sunny days everyone is out playing. But days like this, where the showers scare the masses, this is when you find the real players. By 9 AM I'm sitting outside of the clubhouse, waiting for my chance to play. The partners, they pose no risk to my game. As they proudly inform me they're beginners. I respond by saying I really am not that good. Players like these are much more enjoyable. Many good players seem to believe you play against others. In reality, it is only you against yourself. You can't *beat* someone else in golf like you can in a race. There are no winners or losers, just players. Secondly, new players enjoy the game more. They remind people like myself that mistakes happen and not to take yourself too seriously. In good time we start off, and dark clouds come across the open fairways to foretell an upcoming shower.

The game starts well. I have some good holes. The greens were cut early, and the fairways are fairly wide. My game has been good so far. Not that I would count my scores. You can't get overconfident in golf. Professional players, nine out of ten, will tell you their best day was when they were concentrating on a riddle, a book—something that kept their mind off golf. There's only one time when you should be thinking of golf—when you're hitting the ball.

I'm swinging the clubs well. My shoulders and hands are relaxed, and I'm swinging smoothly. My pre-shot routine is in good order. I've kept it fairly short, while still maintaining consistency. A good pre-shot routine analyzes your current position: how the golf ball is lying on the ground, the distance to the hole, obstacles in the way. You find the direction you want to hit to, and, if important, the ball flight. Then you simply take a few practice swings and hit the ball. A good pre-shot routine focuses you on the task at hand, and nothing else.

Unfortunately my putting is off. My good short iron shots [within 100 yards] have been solid, leaving me on the green earlier, but with longer putts. My playing partners note just how important each of these putts is. Instead of focusing on the putt, I've thought of the joy of making a birdie. By the time we've reached the 8th hole, the rain has started, leaving a nice cooling sensation.

My playing frustrations continue on the next hole. Golf is all about balances. You find your putting isn't working, you try and force an extra long drive or a real aggressive pin shot. These risks, they put you in an even worse state: the breakdown. I follow this through the 12th hole, where I pull my tee shot into the left trees. My ball is in a horrible lie. My pre-shot routine had some problems. I have only one option. I am a sizable distance from the hole, considering taking the bump and run, a low shot that goes low and far toward the hole. But it isn't safe. So, I regrettably take a one shot penalty and bring the ball back into play. Right there I decide I will not lose to the course. I won't put myself in a position to fail. From there I take a solid shot over onto the green, to the surprise of my playing partners.

The safe play saves my round, and although I double-bogey the hole, I par the next. A great tee shot and a confident putt brings me back into playing great golf. I play the next few holes without rashness or fear. This leaves me to the final hole, the 18th. A long par 5, it requires good shots. A solid tee-shot leaves me in light grass. My second shot is a great one, launching the ball low and far. I finish off my approach with a high strike that lands hard on the green and rolls to its current distance from the hole. Had it landed softly, it would've been an easy putt. But the ball doesn't bounce the right way, or at least the way I want it to.

Now as I look at it, the path seems to be slightly straighter than I originally perceived and quite fast. I stand up for the final time, making a mental note on a small leaf at which to aim. I set my putter down after two practice strokes and stand up to the ball. I pull the club back slowly, smoothly and with only slight natural imperfections. As I draw the club down, the shoulders hinge down in harmony. At contact, the leaf blows away with a swift kick. My follow-through hinges off course, hitting the ball with off speed and poor direction. It slides down and rolls perfectly, directly at the hole. I watch in amazement as the ball rolls toward the upcoming cup. It slows down at its approach. I raise my putter in excitement, watching it disappear into the hole. My partners are too stunned to respond. They give me encouragement, reinforcing how great a shot it was. I thank them for their company, and look back at the putt. Yeah, it sank, but I got lucky. Next time I'll do better, and the time after that? Well we'll see. But stick to the task at hand.

Nicole Tardiff

Silently Screaming

1.

I feel like everything is dying around me

My family, My friends, My world
Or is it something inside of Me?
Is it something I'm too blind to see?
When I look into the mirror, what I once saw was not so bad,
But now when I look in the mirror what I find is something so sad
The girl who's looking back at me, although she does not speak a word
I can tell she has a lot to say
Because I have noticed that her smile has begun to fade

I just don't feel the same anymore
Nothing seems to be right
I try to hold my head up high but it always ends up hanging toward the floor
Before my friends told me they hated me
Before My mother's boyfriend, Ron, and all the deaths
I was living such a perfect life
I was actually trying my best.
My sky has turned to a darkened gray
My dreams are no longer real
I have no idea what to believe anymore

I don't know what to feel
My angel left me long ago and I can't seem to find where she went
She has left a special part of me so dreary and upset
I hadn't done anything wrong I was still the same old me
Still I had no answers what in God's name could it be
I sat and thought what I could have possibly said or done
To make my friends so upset with me, to make our friendship come undone

Finally I had an answer, I actually knew what was wrong
With my sickly jealous friends. Why had it taken me so long?
Why couldn't they just be happy for me
They wanted what I had, To be happy just like me
Because they had never experienced the feeling of being free
Now I don't have to worry those insecure Children are out of my life

But it does not end there no not just yet
There is more to the story, More pain and strife

My mother is going through her own loss
I don't know how to help her, I have never taken charge before and been
the boss
She sleeps all the time and says she doesn't care
But I know she still cares about me, for I'm still her little Baby Bear

I still hate to see her suffer
She is the strongest person I know
And it crushes me inside to see her no longer glow
She will get through this and I'm right by her side
And as soon as that day comes we are going to take off and fly
But for now I'm silently screaming at myself and to the world
What no one seems to understand is that for now I'm a lost and lonely little girl.

2.

I can't explain
the feeling I get

when I go to
a Red Sox
baseball game.
It's like this
BANG of energy that rushes through my veins.
I'm free.
No one
can tell me
what to do.

The air is filled with
the spices of
hot dogs, pizza,
Fenway freshly cut grass.
I love it.

Here
everyone is like me,
cheering on my fave
Red Sox players.
I'm not different.
Here
I fit in.

Patrick Trometer

The Life Cycle Of Adam Darren Divise

Early years
book to book to toy to toy
to art to art to art
got tired of reading
got tired of playing
got tired of getting tired

my boat my boat my little toy boat
it broke it broke it broke
my mom my dad
too bad too bad
don't worry don't worry don't worry

to bed to bed to bed too late
too early too early too early
I always remember my waking and sleeping
my worrying my hurrying my speed

Second grade
book to book to paper to paper
to gym to gym to gym
got tired of reading
got tired of writing
got tired of getting tired

my pencil my pencil my big fat pencil
it broke it broke it broke
my teacher my tutor
too bad too bad
I'm worried I'm worried I'm worried

to school to school to school too late
too early too early too early
I always remember my hating and dreading
my worrying my crying my illness

Thirdgraderitalin
test to test to project to project
to quiz to quiz to quiz
got tired of studying
visited a doctor
who tested and tested and tested

I got medicine and help
made a change in my life.
For once I was slower and active.
For once I was glad to be attentive, and
For once I was calm and peaceful
my insides weren't jittery
my outsides were still
my brain was focused
and all from the pill.

I'm better at things
and not always worried.
I'm glad that I got tested
so that I'm not distracted.

Ryan Tsou

A Sixteen-Year-Old's Wisdom

I remember the day I was told that we were planning on moving. It had something to do with my dad's job taking us to Boston. I didn't have an idea that it would become Lexington, but instead I thought "Massachusetts" and "New England." This prospect had been thrown around earlier, so we had already traveled to Boston before. I enjoyed whenever Boston was mentioned because I would think of the "-ahs" of the New England tongue. Moving didn't seem important then; I mean there were still months ahead of me before we were actually packing our bags and going. The idea of moving was about as important as what was last night's dinner. I ate it up fast and that was that.

At the time, life was good, and when I look back, I see myself with friends that were the greatest buddies ever. They had looked upon my moving as a sad situation but still far ahead as well. We would still hang out whenever we could, and things were the same. Dynamic changes did not occur until school was over. The coming of summer vacation meant the coming of the move and soon movers came to our house. They packed large boxes and seemed like big towering beasts to me. I saved some clothes and some stuff I wanted to bring to my friend's house because I was not about to go to Boston with my parents yet. Searching for a house and living in a hotel for a few months wasn't my idea of a good time, and I had some last minute catching up to do with all my friends.

So that's how it was for most of the summer. I was homeless but would be picked up by some friends for a couple of weeks. Then another friend would hang out with me before "I was gone" so I would go to their house and stay there for a while. Fun is the total understatement of these great days. Movies, games, and just chatting for long hours: we did everything. When I look back upon them, these memories are those that I hold closest to my heart. All the while I did my nomadic thing, my parents had traveled to Boston and lived in the hotel searching daily for the right town and the right house. Days went by like this and I was running out of time, as I had to go to Boston. School was starting for my friends soon, and good lucks but no good byes were said as I was sent to the airport.

After my parents met me at the airport in Boston, we returned to the hotel as still, after months of searching, a house was not found. The hotel actually was very nice. It was at a Residence Inn, one of those hotels where long stays are fine since the rooms are stocked with a refrigerator and stove. The hotel was comfy, though after the first week I became sick of it. School wouldn't start for weeks and already I longed to go back to my friends.

Soon we found a house, and Lexington would be my new home. We walked into the colonial styled house, choked at its price and finally decided to take it since after all it was Lexington, and my parents had heard good things.

The house was older than me, smelled funny, and had ugly wallpaper. My parents had decided on a renovation project that unfortunately included much of the house. Loud noises and banging, not to mention dust flying everywhere, created a genuine construction site, and I was left to handle the wallpaper. Scraping off the walls and later painting dominated my lackluster life. When we retreated back to the hotel after a day's work, I would immediately logon to the Internet, my savior. Instantly, I was connected with my friends again six hundred miles away.

The house took forever to become what it is today, but once it was livable, we moved out of the hotel and got situated in our new, renovated, old colonial. It was nice to have my own room again and all of our stuff was moved in, out from three-month storage. When our house finally began to take a nice shape, school was coming up. I had gone to the new-kid orientation program; it made me feel better, but truthfully, being the new kid is strange and uncomfortable. I entered the auditorium on the first day of school lonely, feeling that the whole world was far away. I didn't see any familiar faces and quickly wanted the day to end. Because the first day was the freshmen orientation half-day, it did end quickly though it didn't seem that way at the time. I went home in silence and remembered when my parents asked, "How was school?" The answer was "Bad."

School didn't appeal to me for some time. I mean no one enjoys tests and homework, plus it doesn't help when you don't know anyone at school. After school, I fell back to my online sanctuary. Six hundred miles were nothing with instant messaging, yet it was not the same. Just the knowing that my friends weren't nearby or that I couldn't just call them over hit me hard. I regretted not hanging out with my friends more often and not thanking them for being great friends. I felt bad for not connecting more, and I was afraid friendships would fade. School was tedious and painful, not helping my situation.

In time I began to make new friends, and things began to brighten. This positive aspect of moving was great as I realized that by meeting more and more people my list of great buddies would grow. Now when I think about it, if I hadn't moved I wouldn't know my friends here, and to me that would be the greatest loss. I learned the importance of friendship from both my old and new friends. I also began to see how much value true friendship holds. Moving brought me times of pain, but it also benefited me as I gained new friends and insights of friendship. From now on, I remember to value my friends and thank them for everything they do for me. Thank your friends, and show them you care. Maybe you'll get something out of my experience; I hope you do. I hope you take my advice, but whatever, you know—it's just a sixteen-year-old's wisdom.

Samira Vachani

A Train Ride With A Boy From New York

We sit on the train
Silence within us
Five altogether
Across from each other

Avert our eyes, pretend to smile
We've known each other so well
act as if uneasiness is a choice
Though we know that's a lie

Standing on the platform
Laughing, joking
We were the friends
We've always been

Now we're tense and clumsy
Don't know how to act
Like strangers meeting
For the first time

It's all his fault
That boy from New York
He sits next to me
Tall, rich, and cocky

We got him at South Station
Earlier in the day
We never see each other
Yet wait the forty minutes
Till he saunters in late

A guest from New York
We act polite
Wait for our stop
With no conversation
To wile away time

So busy at school
No time for each other
Too busy to remember
That we've forgotten each other

I smile and nod
At his endless chatter
Why do I hate him
He's good looking enough
Nice and polite

Can someone so simple
makes us forget
The feeling of being together
that we can't seem to get

Whose fault is it
we don't want to answer
It could be ourselves
It's easier to blame him

"Prudential Center"
the intercom sputters
We file out the train
sigh with relief

He makes a joke
I laugh with ease
Suddenly we're all laughing
Maybe I don't mind him

A stranger inside
looks out the window
Follows our path
away from the train

Confused for a moment
Says to herself
"I thought they were strangers"
Maybe she's right.

Andrew Vesprini

ANGER

Anger at school,
Anger at home.
Anger in my life,
Wherever I may go.
It's a feeling that gets at you and grows,
Until your brain full explodes,
You can't take it anymore you can't take it alone,
Can't take it at school nor at home,
School packed with kids and rules like a prison,
Makes you wonder why you even bother,
Dazing off in class thinking of home,
I get home to find nothing but work,
I can't sit still nor do my homework unless music is playing,
I don't know why but that's just the feeling,
Don't have the patience to deal with ignorant people,
Which is why I find myself getting in trouble over and over again.

Alice Wang

Who Am I?

Who am I?
Just a lone teenager standing in the world
Watching life spin around
Wondering where I belong, where my place is
What the world should know me as
What I should see as

Who do others see me as?
A girl
A child
A student
A skater
A dancer
I'm all these
Yet they see only an outer shell

Perhaps my true self is for me and only me to know
I am all the above
Yet there is more
Only I think my thoughts
Only I experience my own life's pleasures
Only I endure my troubles
Only I feel my pains
Only I can follow my heart

Who am I?
I am me
As no one else will ever know
Just me

Warren

The Man

When I got out of the car at the Rotary Barbecue, I could smell the mix of the propane gas and barbecue sauce. The tables on the left were covered with cloths, and on the right were the different stands of competing rib places. I sat with my family at a table. Everyone was there including two uncles' families and my grandmother. The day was sunny and nice, and it was warm like the perfect spring day. The first thing I got to eat was french fries and a lemonade. The french fries weren't just any fried potatoes; they were big, golden brown and crispy on the outside and soft on the inside, steak fries. The lemonade was great because they grabbed a whole lemon and put it into the machine and juiced it out. The only bad thing was when you sucked up one of those big lemon seeds into your mouth, it was gross. My brother and I always looked forward to this because we got to have the lemonade. The different stands had a bunch of different foods to choose from. You could have baby back ribs, country ribs, pulled pork, corn, you name it, they had it. I ate everything and felt full and satisfied. As the day went on, it cooled down a little, so we decided to leave just before it got dark. My mom, brother, and I were clearing out, and my dad said he wanted to stay and help clean up.

At home I went to bed. The phone rang around 12:30 and my mom answered it. I woke up when the phone rang and looked at my red digital clock that let me know it was late. My mom came into the room and told me that she was going to pick up my father. I told her I wanted to go with her. My brother kept sleeping. I really wasn't sure why we were picking up my father until I got to the site of the Barbecue. There were about four other guys with him. I wasn't really paying attention to what their faces looked like, I was focusing on my dad. He didn't want to leave when my mom went up to him to tell him to come. After a few minutes of strong negotiations on my mother's part, he got into the car. I noticed he was asking weird questions and figured he was just joking around.

When we got back to the house, I thought he was still joking when he was walking up the driveway because he was wobbling around and saying weird things I had never heard him say before. We got him upstairs, and it was then I realized he wasn't joking when he laid on his bed and went right to sleep. I still didn't know what was wrong. It wasn't till a few years later that I thought back on that incident and realized that he was drunk. I lost some respect for my dad, and I thought that there was nothing good about alcohol if that could happen to my dad who had always been "The Man."

Brian Woods

A Small Cheer

The ocean breeze
felt good across
my sunburned face.

I felt a tug
on the fishing pole
but it was only there

for a moment. "The damn thing
stole my bait!" I yelled.
Captain Lou cracked open a beer

and tossed me a Coke. He came over
to assist me and to hook the worm.
After a few minutes

the pole suddenly
jerked out at almost
a 90-degree angle.

I reeled in a 32-inch bass
and earned a small cheer.
It was my birthday

and all my friends were here.
We all cracked open our Cokes
and headed back to the port and

before I knew it we were already there.

Liz Yurkevich

If You Only Knew

If you only knew when I heard your first song,
All I could do was sit and listen.
I wondered that in my life so far,
If you were the five guys I was missing.

If you only knew that when I saw you perform
For the first time on TV,
My entire being was in awe of you,
It was such a thrill for me.

If you only knew I've traveled far and wide,
To see you on your tour.
I had the time of my life at the shows,
They left me wanting more.

If you only knew how each of your songs,
Makes me look forward to every day.
The positive lyrics and melodies
Chase all my bad thoughts away.

If you only knew how you dress
And the way you comb your hair,
Drives me so out of my mind,
That all I can do is stare.

If you only knew when I hear you sing,
My heart always skips a beat.
It sends chills up and down my spine,
And makes me want to move my feet.

If you only knew how your smiles brighten my room,
With all the posters I've collected on the wall.
I know that I only have to look to you,
To make sure I never fall.

If you only knew how you've inspired me
To become the person I am today.
I've overcome so many obstacles,
And my skies are never gray.

If you only knew that underneath your image,
And all the money and fame,
You will always be the young men you were before,
You will always stay the same.

If you only knew how much time I spent,
Thinking out your letter.
I wanted to make sure it was perfect,
Since you've changed my life for the better.

If you only knew I want to thank you,
For all you've given me in the past.
I know that after all these years,
My dedication to you is meant to last.

If you only knew how you've shown me
That all my dreams can come true.
I've found what I love in life,
And I owe it all to you.

If you only knew how millions love you,
But I want to be different from the rest.

I want to be that one fan you'll remember,
And maybe even call your best.

If you only knew I watch from far away
Supporting everything you do.
I wish you knew I existed,
And how I do everything for you.

If you only knew my name.

0-595-24797-0